Best Teams

Best Teams

Creating and Maintaining High-Performing Teams

By Marc Woods

CAPSTONE
A Wiley Brand

Registered Offices
John Wiley & Sons, Inc., 111 River Street, Hoboken, NJ 07030, USA
John Wiley & Sons Ltd, New Era House, 8 Oldlands Way, Bognor Regis, West Sussex, PO22 9NQ, UK

For details of our global editorial offices, customer services, and more information about Wiley products visit us at www.wiley.com.

The manufacturer's authorized representative according to the EU General Product Safety Regulation is Wiley-VCH GmbH, Boschstr. 12, 69469 Weinheim, Germany, e-mail: Product_Safety@wiley.com.

Wiley also publishes its books in a variety of electronic formats and by print-on-demand. Some content that appears in standard print versions of this book may not be available in other formats.

Library of Congress Cataloging-in-Publication Data

Names: Woods, Marc, author.
Title: Best teams : creating and maintaining high-performing teams / Marc Woods.
Description: Hoboken, NJ : Wiley, 2026. | Includes index.
Identifiers: LCCN 2025037361 (print) | LCCN 2025037362 (ebook) | ISBN 9781394249701 (paperback) | ISBN 9781394249725 (adobe pdf) | ISBN 9781394249718 (epub)
Subjects: LCSH: Teams in the workplace. | Performance.
Classification: LCC HD66 .W6745 2026 (print) | LCC HD66 (ebook)
LC record available at https://lccn.loc.gov/2025037361
LC ebook record available at https://lccn.loc.gov/2025037362

Cover Design: Wiley
Cover Image: © Ariestia/stock.adobe.com

Set in 10/14pt and Montserrat by Straive, Chennai, India.
Printed and bound by CPI Group (UK) Ltd, Croydon, CR0 4YY

C9781394249701_060925

In memory of Brainy Steve.

*A beloved part of my team whose humour and support
are deeply missed.*

Contents

Acknowledgements

Being ahead of schedule with this project means, for once, I can more carefully consider who I would like to acknowledge.

First, thank you to my publishers Wiley, who keep coming back for more, particularly Annie Knight, Alice Hadaway, Laura Cooksley and Venkat Sankar, who were closest to this project.

The decision to give the contributors a clear voice in the book means I am delighted to introduce Sally Munday, Helen Webb, Charles Conn, Simon Lambert, Yvette Edwards, Dan Futter, Andreas Schierenbeck, Caoimhe Keogan, Noelle Perkins, Andria Vidler, Alim Dhanji, Pedro de la Rosa and Matt Parker. They all gave their time and insights so generously.

If I ever had a superpower, it's the ability to surround myself with people infinitely more capable than myself. My organisational psychologist friends are a great example of this, so thank you Mandip Johal, Laura Heron and Prachee Luthra for both your guidance and checking the veracity of my Best Teams model. Thank you also to Sandy Ogg for generously contributing the Foreword for this book.

Georgia Kirke and Delphine Hanton did a wonderful job of testing my thinking and its application in the business world.

Finally, for her editing and writing skills, Kat Lewis has been a delight to work with, joining forces with me when I wasn't entirely sure I wanted to write again. Without Kat, I would appear much less erudite.

Unfortunately, being ahead of schedule doesn't necessarily mean I will have remembered everyone so just in case—thank you to anyone else who knows me.

Foreword
by Sandy Ogg

I first met Marc in 2021, when we were both supporting a client through some significant changes in their business. My area of expertise is what I call finding the 'click'—that magical place where an individual's unique talents match unequivocally with the work they are asked to complete in the role in which they've been placed.

On this project, I focused on the required changes to their executive leadership operating model to drive alignment and value creation for the enterprise. Marc worked on the team dynamics and assisted the client to embed their highly valued leadership behaviour code. Our differing areas of expertise aligned well to provide the 'click' in this situation, and we deployed our unique talents to everyone's advantage.

During this time, Marc and I also bonded over our love of sports and developed a mutual admiration of one another's ability to deliver meaningful impact in both changing and challenging situations.

When Marc shared his Best Teams Model with me, I could immediately see its value. Having worked with CEOs and C-suite executives for over 30 years, and served in that position myself, I know that achieving high performance and real impact at both a team and organisational level is very tough and yet, it makes the difference between business success and failure. But it can be equally tough to define the secret sauce that drives teams to bring out the best from themselves and others to create outsized value for their organisation.

In *Best Teams*, Marc breaks this concept down into 12 measurable attributes and, in doing so, gives leaders everywhere a blueprint to guide them on their own journeys to high performance.

But more than that, in this book, he brings in the perspectives of leaders from a range of world-leading organisations. Their insights, presented alongside the Best Teams Model, offer a fantastic foundation on which to build high-performing, result-driven teams in any industry.

While each of the attributes Marc outlines are important on their own, their true value comes from bringing them together. Creating value is the underlying goal for any CEO or executive leader, and this book moves the needle in the right direction for sure. As the rate of external change continues to far outpace the rate of internal change in organisations, we need all the tools possible to deliver that value and win in the marketplace. Make *Best Teams* part of your toolkit and unlock new levels of performance and impact in your organisation.

Sandy Ogg
Founder, CEO.works
Host of the *Sandy on Talent* podcast

Introduction

I'd like to start by asking you two simple questions: What would happen if you and your team could become the best at what you do? And, perhaps more importantly, once you are, how can you sustain that level of performance?

What would happen in your team will be a deeply personal answer. Perhaps you'll improve the financial performance of the business, or maybe you'll significantly improve customer service. You may even be measuring your success based on the hiring and retention of the best people in your industry. The metrics that demonstrate success to you will be different from every other person reading this book, because no two people and no two teams are the same.

Where I can help is by showing you how to achieve that level of performance in the first instance, and providing you with the tools you need to maintain a high-performing team thereafter. I'll talk more about what a high-performing team is, and share an overview of my Best Teams Model in the coming two chapters.

For now, I'd like you to take a moment to bring your focus inwards and think about how you show up as a leader. What do you currently do to support your team's performance? And if you're honest with yourself, what could you do better? Because the truth is that no team can achieve high performance without a leader who is just as dedicated to this outcome as everyone else on the team.

I ask these questions not to make you feel bad, but to help you flex your all-important self-awareness muscle. Simply by picking up this book, you've demonstrated that you know things aren't as good as they could be in your team. That's great—because seeking out tools like my Best Teams Model is the first step towards positive change.

As we move through the coming chapters, all I ask is that you approach each with an open mind. Lean into what you don't know and remain curious. Encourage your teams to do the same and you're off to a good start.

But why should you listen to me? I've spent 25 years working as an executive leadership coach, and during that time, I have encountered many high-performing teams, as well as some that definitely fell at the other end of the spectrum. It's through this experience, as well as my 16 years as a professional swimmer and Paralympic athlete, that I have developed my Best Teams Model. This model outlines the three main elements that I believe all high-performing teams have in common, along with the 12 attributes that contribute to delivering true high performance in any setting.

Before we dive into what I mean by high performance in more detail, there are two things I'd like you to bear in mind:

1. There are no quick fixes to deliver high performance. This is a process that takes time and effort, and it is one that will never be finished. As a leader, it's

your role to equip every individual on your teams with the tools they need to constantly drive for high performance, and to provide them with an environment that enables them to bring their best selves to work every day.

2. My Best Teams Model is like a compass that can guide you on this journey, but it isn't a tick-box exercise. Each of the 12 attributes are intrinsically linked, and it is only when you have all of them working in harmony that you will achieve true high performance as a team. What you do well and what needs work can and will change within your team over time. Embrace this process, and simply return to the model whenever things feel as though they have slipped out of alignment.

As you move through the chapters, you'll not only hear from me but also from 13 incredible organisational leaders who have generously shared their insights on the specific attributes included in the model, and on the ecosystem of a high-performing team as a whole. I hope that you find their practical insights, as well as the exercises at the end of each chapter, valuable as you create and then maintain your own high-performing team.

Let's get started.

1

What is a High-Performing Team?

The phrase 'high-performing team' is prevalent in business circles, and with good reason. What leader wants a low-performing team after all? Many businesses have average-performing teams that do what's required but little more. And then there are high-performing teams, the ones that stand head and shoulders above the rest.

Every leader wants to have a high-performing team, but what does that look like?

If you take the time to consider truly great teams, you might find yourself thinking of the 1990s Chicago Bulls basketball team, within which Michael Jordan was a central figure, or perhaps Microsoft under the leadership of Bill Gates. Although these teams contained well-known names, those individuals alone could not have achieved even half of what they did without the support of those around them. These teams worked collaboratively towards exceptional results, sharing clear objectives, communicating openly and fostering a culture of trust and respect among members.

Michael Jordan would not have achieved so much without his teammates like Dennis Rodman, Scottie Pippin and Toni Kukoč, not to mention the Bulls' head coach Phil Jackson directing from off the court. Nor would Bill Gates have been able to lead Microsoft to such great heights had he not valued the contributions of those across every team and level at the organisation. He recognised that a team of the best people working closely together could achieve far more than he ever could alone.

I have been observing the attributes of high-performing teams for many years and have realised that they are all underpinned by three central elements. They have people who feel empowered, they have clearly defined processes and they nurture supportive cultures.

But what is it about those three elements that makes them crucial to creating and maintaining high-performing teams?

I always begin by focusing on empowered people. We need to acknowledge that high-performing teams consist of individuals with unique strengths collaborating seamlessly with one another. This was one of Gates' greatest strengths as a leader. Each member should have a strong work ethic, be given autonomy, have integrity and a growth mindset.

However, talented individuals on their own aren't enough to create a high-performing team. These talented individuals need to be supported and guided by clearly defined processes to ensure that tasks are completed with precision and consistency. Even in the modern world of working, where flexibility is prized by many, teams still need structure. High-performing teams have established processes which ensure that high-quality communication, goal setting, accountability and recognition are consistently delivered throughout the organisation.

Finally, there is the glue that holds it all together, namely a nurturing and supportive culture. Within a high-performance culture, members feel valued, respected and supported. They are, therefore, more likely to communicate openly, take ownership of their work and collaborate effectively. High-performing teams prioritise cultivating a culture of resilience, psychological safety, inclusion and a One Team Ethos.

Although I have broken the components of a high-performing team down into the three crucial elements of empowered people, defined processes and a supportive culture, the truth is that these three elements are deeply intertwined. You'll not only notice this within my Best Teams Model (see Figure 1.1), but also hear how these elements interact in the real world through the leaders I've interviewed for this book.

Before we go any further, take a minute to consider your team. Do you have any of these elements in place? Perhaps you have all three and, if you do, are you consistently reviewing them to ensure that your team continues to operate at its optimum?

Figure 1.1 The elements of the Best Teams Model

The Business Case for High-Performing Teams

Creating high-performing teams is more than a nice-to-have. It's a business imperative. The business case for high-performing teams feels intuitive, but there is also hard evidence, which backs up how high-performing teams provide a powerful advantage for both companies and employees.

Let's start with the obvious measures: productivity and profitability.

According to research undertaken by Gallup, highly engaged teams are 21% more profitable than their less engaged counterparts. Additionally, such teams achieve 17% higher productivity and a 41% decrease in absenteeism, which can have a direct positive impact on an organisation's operational effectiveness and financial health.[1]

But it doesn't stop there. When your organisation is made up of high-performing teams, your customers also tend to be happier. Research shows that engaged and high-performing teams directly enhance customer loyalty. In fact, companies with high employee engagement report a 233% greater rate of customer loyalty.[2] Of course, customer loyalty has a positive impact on a business' bottom line.

But high-performing teams don't only help your organisation make more money, they also prevent you from losing money. Analysis by the Project Management Institute (PMI) found that high-performing organisations that use proven project, program and portfolio management practices (in other words have defined processes in their businesses) see their projects meeting their goals and business intent 2.5 times more frequently than other organisations. What's more, these high-performing companies waste 13 times *less* money than their lower-performing counterparts.[3]

So, if you have high-performing teams in your organisation, not only are they likely to get more work done, but they are also likely to help your business earn more money. The question then becomes, what do you need to do to embed those three overarching elements in your teams?

2

The Best Teams Model

At the heart of my Best Teams Model are the three essential elements I identified in the previous chapter: empowered people, defined processes and supportive culture. However, underneath each of these elements sit four attributes that feed into empowering people, creating defined processes and developing a supportive culture.

These are the tangible skills and attributes you can work on as an individual and collectively to help create high-performing teams within your organisation.

In each of the following chapters, I'll explore an attribute in turn. I'll share real-world examples of individuals and companies that have nailed an attribute, and I'll provide you with exercises and tools that you can use yourself and with your teams to improve in each area. Before we dive into the attributes in detail, here's an overview of them and how they feed into those three essential elements of empowered people, defined processes and supportive culture (see Figure 2.1).

Figure 2.1 The attributes of the Best Teams Model

Attributes for Empowered People

Richard Branson famously once noted that 'people are your greatest asset'. That might sound a bit cheesy, but it's true. Businesses simply don't function without people, and they certainly don't excel without great people who feel empowered in their roles. That's why the first element of the Best Teams Model is all about the people in your organisation.

During the years I have spent working with and observing high-performing teams, I've noticed that the people within these teams have four key attributes that help them to feel empowered and therefore to do their best work:

- Work ethic

- Autonomy

- Integrity

- Growth mindset.

Often the first thing you will notice within high-performing teams is the *work ethic*. People are reliable, consistently meet deadlines and deliver a high standard of work. When leaders encourage a strong work ethic, people collaborate effectively, offer support and assistance and contribute constructively to group efforts.

While you can try to enforce a strong work ethic on a team, this isn't sustainable. You need to build a team who want to work hard and support one another, not one where you constantly have to crack the whip. As a leader, the best way to do that is by giving each member of the team a degree of independence in their work.

When you give top performers *autonomy*, they are able to make decisions in the moment and drive to their goals more efficiently. People who are given autonomy are more self-aware, engaged, motivated and committed to continuously improve performance.

One study in 2020 found that giving people autonomy at work increased their productivity by 5.2% and had a significant positive impact on their mood.[1] Another survey carried out by Effectory in 2019 revealed that those who have autonomy at work have greater clarity over their role, are more engaged and committed to their work and report higher satisfaction and alignment with their jobs.[2] All of this leads to higher performance.

Integrity is the next attribute you will see among individuals in high-performing teams. This means there is honesty, openness and trust amongst team members, all of which are essential for those in your team to benefit from having greater autonomy at work.

Trust is particularly important for individuals, teams and organisations. Deloitte's research shows that employees who trust their employers are 260% more motivated to work and have 41% lower rates of absenteeism than those who don't trust the organisation they work for.[3] Of course, trust is a two-way street.

Leaders set the tone for behaviour and performance within the team. Demonstrating integrity inspires others to do the same. When you foster a culture of honesty, openness and trust within your team, you will see significant benefits in terms of team performance.

Finally, members of high-performing teams contribute to a culture of continuous learning as they seek opportunities for growth and to develop new skills. They have a *growth mindset*, both individually and collectively. By being encouraged to stay curious, a team is more likely to innovate and drive organisational excellence.

Attributes for Defined Processes

Defined processes are like the guardrails that enable you to give people greater autonomy. These processes also help individuals to work more effectively and encourage them to develop their growth mindset. The attributes required to create valuable defined processes are:

- Communication
- Accountability
- Goal setting
- Recognition.

Communication is the bedrock of any high-performing team. Effective leaders communicate a vision and expectations. They also feedback clearly and consistently. Planning communications ensures that people understand their roles, responsibilities and objectives, and it enables informed decision-making.

Research from Grammarly in 2023 found that the top three benefits of effective communication were increased productivity, increased customer satisfaction and increased employee confidence.[4] Leaders can't leave communication to chance—it is a skill that needs to be honed and an activity that needs to be planned to ensure that it is used effectively.

Clear and structured communication and feedback mechanisms, along with the attributes covered under empowered people, allow leaders to hold those on their teams *accountable*.

When individuals take ownership and are held accountable for their actions and results, they strive for excellence and contribute to the team's success. Creating performance management processes helps monitor progress and identify areas for improvement.

However, it is very difficult to hold people accountable for their output if they do not have a clear and defined goal to work towards. This holds true whether you are talking about individual or team accountability.

Establishing clear, *measurable goals* aligned with organisational objectives provides focus and direction for teams. Defining project management processes, including project scopes, priorities, timelines and resource allocations, ensures efficient execution.

Research by PwC found that individuals who set at least four daily goals per week at work were 34% more likely to achieve their key performance indicators (KPIs) than those who didn't set daily goals, and they were happier in their jobs.[5] This research specifically focused on the power of small goals. Just imagine how setting clear team and organisational goals, while encouraging individuals to set daily goals, could positively impact your team's performance.

The final attribute under defined processes is *recognition*. Recognising the contributions of team members boosts morale, motivation and commitment. Defining a system for reward and recognition drives engagement and performance. As we'll explore later, recognition comes in many forms and often financially costs nothing despite having a significant positive impact on performance.

Attributes for A Supportive Culture

The final element in the Best Teams Model is culture. The four key attributes that feed into creating a supportive culture are:

- Resilience

- Inclusion

- Psychological safety

- One Team Ethos.

Nurturing a culture of adaptability and *resilience* prepares teams to navigate change, uncertainty and adversity— all of which is particularly important in the 21st century where change is happening more rapidly and uncertainty is near constant. Being resilient also encourages teams to respond quickly to challenges, seize opportunities and drive continuous improvement. As with many of these attributes, individual resilience is just as important as team resilience and shouldn't be overlooked.

Our resilience at work can be impacted by the next attribute: *inclusion*. Embracing diversity, equity and inclusion creates a culture where different perspectives, backgrounds and experiences are valued and respected. This improves the sense of belonging employees feel and promotes mutual understanding among team members. It's important to note that while diversity and equity are important, inclusion stands separately to those two things. You can have an incredibly diverse team, but if people within that team feel excluded, they will never achieve high performance.

There is a great deal of data about the benefits of creating an inclusive workplace, but one of the most striking statistics I've come across from a business perspective is that inclusive teams make better business decisions 87% of the time, and make decisions twice as fast as non-inclusive teams.[6] Creating an inclusive environment feeds into many of the attributes of high-performing teams, and when you get this right, it can have a significant positive impact across the board.

Inclusion is, naturally, essential for the next attribute on the list: *psychological safety*. Environments where psychological safety is prioritised allow team members to take risks, share ideas and express concerns without fear of reprisal. This fosters open communication, candid feedback and innovation.

Finally, by encouraging collaboration and consistency, a culture of 'we are all in this together' is created. Sharing best practice and taking time to understand the roles of others brings the organisation together under a *One Team Ethos*.

How Do You Score?

Before you continue reading, take some time to score your team on each of the 12 attributes I've just outlined (see Figure 2.2). Use a simple traffic light system—green for smashing it, amber for working on it but could do better, red for way off the mark. Use those scores as a guide for reading this book. You don't have to work through the chapters in a linear fashion. Instead, see which areas you need to work on (the reds) and start there. Addressing these is likely to deliver the greatest impact.

It is also valuable to understand where your strengths as a team lie, so that you can lean on those to help you develop the attributes where you are weaker.

This book is designed to be a tool to help you develop and maintain a high-performing team, so dip in and out of it as you see fit.

If you would like to be a touch more precise with your scoring, take a look at the appendix where you will find definitions for each attribute and a guide to help you consider where your team is at.

Figure 2.2 Your score on the Best Teams Model

Part I

Empowered People

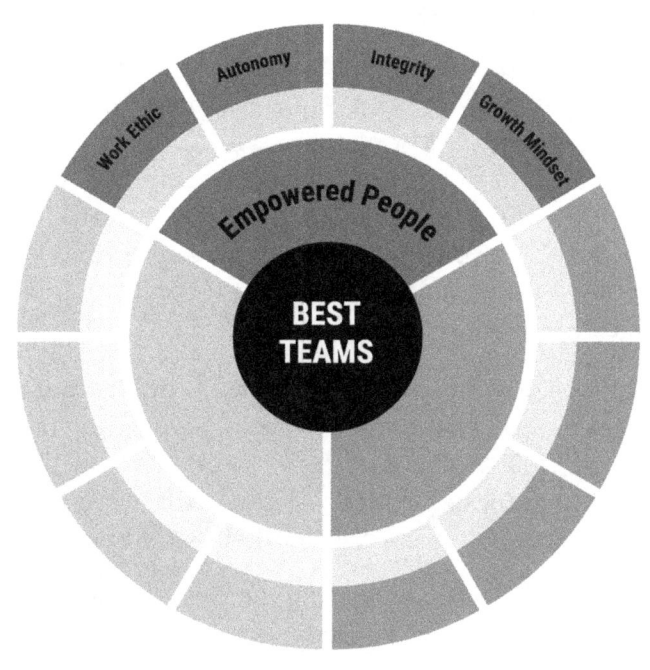

In 2006, the Ford Motor Company was on the verge of bankruptcy, facing declining sales and mounting losses. The company suffered from a siloed structure, a lack of team cohesion and low morale. CEO Alan Mulally recognised that achieving a turnaround required empowering employees to take the initiative.

Mulally implemented the 'One Ford' strategy, which emphasised teamwork, integrity and collective responsibility. Employees were encouraged to take ownership of their work and were given the autonomy to make decisions within their areas of expertise. This approach fostered a strong work ethic, as team members felt accountable for their contributions and committed to the company's success.

A focus on transparency was key to this transformation. Weekly meetings brought leaders together to discuss challenges openly, without fear of retribution, reinforcing integrity and enabling employees to tackle problems collaboratively. Employees also embraced a growth mindset, exploring innovative solutions, such as redesigning vehicles for greater fuel efficiency and incorporating advanced technology.

By 2009, Ford had returned to profitability, becoming the only major US automaker to avoid government bailouts during the financial crisis. Iconic products like the Ford Fusion and Escape symbolised the company's renewed focus on customer needs and market leadership.

Ford's revival under Mulally is a testament to the transformative power of empowerment. By promoting autonomy, cultivating a strong work ethic, upholding integrity and encouraging a growth mindset, Ford's employees overcame immense challenges and positioned the company for sustainable growth and innovation. This story continues to serve as a blueprint for leaders seeking to inspire high-performing, engaged teams.

But Ford is far from the only example of an organisation that empowers its people and, in doing so, achieves success. In the coming chapters, you'll hear from four leaders who embody the attributes that sit under the element of empowered people. I encourage you to use the knowledge and experience that they have so generously shared to help create your own blueprint for empowering your people and building a high-performing team.

3

How Work Ethic Impacts High-Performing Teams

A team can't achieve its potential without the individuals within it having a strong work ethic. They must be diligent, reliable, responsible, professional and dedicated. People with a strong work ethic typically demonstrate a commitment to completing tasks efficiently and effectively, adhering to deadlines, taking initiative, showing accountability for their actions and continuously striving for improvement.

While some people naturally have a strong work ethic, others may find this more of a challenge. The good news is that you can help anyone on a team improve their work ethic if it is not where it needs to be. This is crucial because you need a collectively strong work ethic to succeed as a team.

To sustain a high-performing team, you must remain vigilant and ensure that you aren't carrying anyone who has become 'work-shy'. If you don't address an individual perceived as no longer delivering at an expected level, then others begin to think, 'They aren't working hard, so why should I?'

It's therefore worth considering how to spot people with a poor work ethic. Tell-tale signs may be:

- Deliverables are not being met on time, leading to delays in project completion and potentially disappointing clients or customers.

- Output may be substandard, with errors, omissions or a lack of attention to detail, which can affect the quality of products or services.

- Managers may need to spend more time monitoring and correcting the work of employees with poor work ethics, diverting attention from other vital tasks.

- Other team members may become frustrated or disheartened by their colleagues' poor performance or lack of commitment.

There are ways you can support team members in developing their work ethic. First, though, take a look at yourself. If you don't have a great work ethic, why should they? It's important to lead by example. Assuming you are getting that right, you next have to determine if what might be presenting as poor work ethic is actually that an individual has something else going on in their lives that is distracting them temporarily. If this is the case, talk to them about how you can support them during this time.

If this isn't the issue, however, a good starting point is to ensure that they have meaningful work engaging them. Help them develop self-discipline, prioritise tasks and start the day strongly. It's easier to start strongly and maintain than to enter into the day at a sub-par level and then raise your game.

A word of warning, though: leading people with a strong work ethic also requires emotional intelligence. Investing time in understanding, managing and responding appro-priately to others' emotions will help ensure that people manage their well-being. If you don't, they will eventually either physically or mentally burn out, impacting your team's ability to perform effectively.

As well as examining your own work ethic, take a few minutes to consider your colleagues' work ethic. Could it be improved? What can you do differently to improve their performance or manage their well-being?

Finding the Right Work Ethic Balance

The term 'karoshi', meaning 'death by overwork', emerged in Japan in the 1970s. As the country's economy boomed, a work culture developed around intense loyalty, long hours and the concept of 'lifetime employment'. Karoshi came to describe cases where otherwise healthy employees suffered sudden health issues—typically heart attacks or strokes—attributed directly to overwork and the stress of prolonged, intense hours.

Japanese workers are generally entitled to 10–20 days of paid leave each year, depending on their years of service. However, it is common for employees to take only a fraction of this allowance. Japanese employees take less than half of their allocated leave annually.

It's crucial to clarify that sharing this example does not endorse such extreme work practices but reminds us of the need for balance. When discussing a strong work ethic, it's important to emphasise that output quality should outweigh the sheer volume of hours worked.

Sustainable productivity relies on a balance between hard work and adequate rest. True work ethic is not about working oneself to exhaustion but rather committing to excellence, efficiency and quality—principles that ensure long-term health and productivity for everyone on a team. There are many examples of how this can look—and crucially they are not all the same.

Could You Be More Taylor?

Whether it is her constant desire to write songs, running on a treadmill whilst singing her setlist or performing on 152 dates across five continents on her Eras Tour, Taylor Swift is a grafter.

Taylor Swift's management company directly employs less than 20 people. Still, when you consider the Eras Tour, there are hundreds of people employed across many roles, including promotion, set design and rigging, logistics, six musicians, four backing singers, 15 dancers and a fleet of around 90 trucks to transport equipment, which started moving more than a week before each show. You can be sure Swift's work ethic is apparent to them all, as are the outcomes of all of this hard work.

At the Grammy Awards, she became the first person to win the prize for album of the year four times. At the age of 34, she has had 12 Number One singles in the American Billboard chart.

Swift's success is not confined to music. She collaborates in fashion and has her own line of perfumes. Her mere presence at American football games to watch her boyfriend, Travis Kelce, raised not only his profile but has also been credited with raising NFL viewing figures.

Patrick Mahomes, the Kansas City Quarterback, told *TIME*, 'She's never not working, even when she's taking her downtime, she's working on something. Shooting a music video or singing a song or writing a song. You can see it by how she talks. Even when she's talking about football, when she's learning it, you can see her business mind putting it together. It's almost like she's trying to become a coach. 'Why can't you try this, this, and this?' She's asking the right questions. The Chiefs went from a nationwide team that was kind of global to a full global worldwide team,' Mahomes said. 'That came from Taylor's fanbase'.[1]

The impact on her bank balance was apparent too when in 2024 she entered the Forbes World's Billionaires list for the first time with $1.1bn.

There is an effect beyond her own personal wealth, too. The BBC estimated that the UK leg of the Eras Tour boosted UK spending by almost £1bn in 2024, with more than a million people watching her perform live.[2]

Swift's story epitomises the value of a relentless work ethic and maintaining a strategic focus on continuous growth and innovation. Her success is not merely the result of talent but also sustained effort across many facets of life and work. She consistently puts in the hard work to improve her craft, from writing songs to performing.

Take five minutes to think of one area where you would like to improve your work ethic, and write down at least one action you can consistently take to make that improvement.

Motoring to the Top

Mary Barra's journey to the top of General Motors (GM) is a testament to her relentless work ethic, dedication and willingness to take on tough challenges. Barra began working at GM at age 18, juggling a full-time schedule in the company's engineering department while studying at Kettering University (then General Motors Institute). This early experience gave her a foundational understanding of the company's processes and the automotive industry. Still, it also demanded discipline and commitment to balance hands-on work with rigorous academics.

Throughout her career, Barra worked tirelessly to earn her place at every level. She didn't shy away from roles others might have avoided, including a series of demanding technical and managerial positions that required technical expertise and leadership finesse. Barra's focus on continuous learning and her strong work ethic became even more evident as she earned an MBA from Stanford University while being sponsored by GM. This further solidified her strategic thinking and her value to the company.

As she moved through GM's ranks, Barra took on challenging roles in engineering, manufacturing and human resources, which tested her ability to manage complex operations and lead large teams. Her role in human resources proved pivotal; she focused intensively on streamlining GM's workforce and cultivating a more transparent, collaborative corporate culture. Barra's colleagues noticed her drive to push through these problematic restructuring efforts, as she sought to create a stronger, more unified company that would operate with integrity and efficiency.

Barra's dedication was particularly evident when she was appointed Executive Vice President of Global Product Development, a role requiring intense commitment and attention to detail. In this role, she implemented a more customer-centric approach, overseeing global product strategies and pioneering the development of GM's electric and autonomous vehicle lines. She consistently worked long hours and embraced accountability, often spending late nights at work to ensure product safety and quality. This commitment became even more critical when she assumed the CEO role in 2014.

During her tenure as CEO, Barra faced significant challenges, including navigating GM through a large-scale recall crisis early on. Her handling of this issue was marked by a relentless commitment to transparency and accountability, which required her to work closely with internal and external teams around the clock. Barra's hands-on approach, tireless work ethic and determination to transform GM for the future underscore her success and have set her apart as a leading figure in the automotive industry.

What can you learn that will help you lead more effectively? Where can you gain that knowledge and how can you balance learning something new with your leadership?

In Conversation With Sally Munday, CEO UK Sport

Sally Munday has spent her career working with high-performing teams in the world of sport. Top athletes are often recognised for their work ethic, and this carries into the governing bodies that Sally has been and is part of, which made her the ideal person to speak to about this attribute.

MARC: *How would you describe a strong work ethic?*

SALLY: I would describe a strong work ethic as an approach that is built on a set of values which present as a set of behaviours that can collectively contribute to a strong work ethic. This is why we talk about our values a lot at UK Sport.

But when I think about my 'leadership journey' rather than talking about values I talk about my three anchors, which are integrity, passion and vision. These are the anchors that allow me to operate in the way I operate, and to think about my work in a consistently coherent way. Vision is about having a really clear plan. I'm sure you're familiar with the Peter Drucker quote, 'Culture eats strategy for breakfast,' and while I believe culture is really important, I also believe that you don't have to choose between culture and strategy. You need both. You can have an amazing culture, but if you have no plan, you can just end up being busy fools, albeit happy busy fools.

As well as a strong belief in having clarity of vision and purpose, I believe on a personal level that you should do things you love. The reason passion is really important to me is that we spend an awful lot of our time at work, so you've got to have a care, desire and passion for what you're doing.

Integrity is, I think, really critical. In a leadership role, it's particularly important. All new staff at UK Sport get an hour with me as part of their induction. I talk about strategy during those sessions, but I also talk about our values. In particular, I talk about integrity and the responsibility they have, no matter what their level within the organisation, of being a custodian of leadership because they are working for a leadership body.

But what I find interesting about integrity is that if you asked a room of 10 people, we'd all have a slightly different definition of what that looks like. My definition is having the courage to do what's right, not what's easy. So, when I think about work ethic, I think about how passion, integrity and vision align.

Within an organisation, this looks slightly different. At UK Sport, we have four values, but we've spent a lot of time as a team working out how they come to life. What are the behaviours that we should see? What are our expectations of each other under those values?

For example, one of our values is integrity and openness. Under that value, we have a series of behaviours, such as, 'I'm courageous and always do the right thing, even when it's not easy'; 'I am honest and fair'; 'I'll do what I say, give honest feedback and treat everyone with respect'; 'I am open about how I'm feeling and actively taking responsibility for my own health and well-being'.

MARC: *Does it matter what anchors other people within the organisation have? Or is it less about their specific anchors and more about how comfortably they sit with the values?*

SALLY: As an organisation, we talk about how everyone will have their own values and anchors. Creating a value statement is not about trying to create robots or mini-mes. Everybody's life experiences shape the things that are important to them. But we wanted to be very clear about what working at UK Sport is about, what we can expect of each other and what we want you to expect of yourself. So if you're not being honest with yourself or other people, it's completely reasonable for us to call you out on that—and not just for leaders to do so, but also your peers.

MARC: *When you were CEO at England and GB Hockey, would you say a similar thing played out there?*

SALLY: What's interesting about a high-performing team is that it needs to create its own, as you've called it, 'One Team Ethos'. For example, the women's team sat within the performance unit, which was just one part of England and GB Hockey. But we weren't going to dictate that their team ethos had to be our organisational values. They had to work out what was right for them, within the boundaries of being part of the performance unit in the organisation.

So if they had come up with something that was completely in conflict with our organisational values, then we would have stepped in, but that was never a concern because they had such excellent leadership. What was interesting with the women's programme was that in the 20 years I was at the organisation, I saw it evolve from the point where they didn't even qualify for the Olympics in 2004, right through to winning Olympic Gold in 2016.

MARC: *How did that impact how they operated and how they defined a good work ethic?*

SALLY: In the lead up to 2012, [where they won Bronze] the team had an ethos. Then, between 2012 and 2016, obviously some players went and some new players came in, so they redefined that ethos. They talked about wanting to be the difference, create history and inspire the future—and those were the three things they focused on as a team.

There was a lot of focus on how they showed up every day to be the difference. They asked questions like, 'How do I, as an individual, show up and be the difference to this team being successful?' and

'How can I be the difference when I'm in the gym to help me be better at my role?' If you watch the interview the captain did immediately after winning the Gold medal, she talks about how they wanted to create history and inspire the future—and how they felt they'd achieved that. You could see that ethos running through them in the leadership of the group, not just with the captain.

One of the other things that I think sets apart a high-performing team is their ability to resolve their own issues. They don't necessarily look upwards or outwards, but are able to resolve issues themselves. Their coach enabled and empowered that group of players to deal with a lot of issues themselves, which was really important, but their value about being the difference and a lot of the behaviours they discussed as a result of that were what drove their work ethic and what they were willing to do for each other.

MARC: *That's a fascinating dynamic. One thing I've noticed about my Best Teams Model is that many of the attributes are interconnected. To create that work ethic, you need to resolve things as a group, you need psychological safety, you need empowerment, as you've said. Within UK Sport, what does that work ethic look like on an individual, team and organisational level?*

SALLY: At UK Sport, we treat people like adults, by which I mean we trust them as adults, and we expect and hope that they will trust us.

A good example of how we demonstrate that trust is our parameters around being in the office. There's a lot of chatter in the industry about people going back to the office, but we've not dictated that our people need to be in the office two days a week or four days a week or whatever. Instead, we've consulted with our staff post-COVID about how to enable the organisation to work in the most effective way and therefore how to enable them to work in the most effective way. What came out most strongly from those conversations was the value of in-person time.

Given that we have some staff who are in office roles and others who are out on the road, embedded with sports, what we've said is that we want everyone to have a minimum of 20% of their work time face-to-face. Now, for a lot of our staff, that figure will be 70–80%, because of the nature of their role. But that doesn't mean they've got to be in the office one day a week. We didn't want them to think that after being on the road, they have to go and do their one day in the office, because that doesn't make sense.

So we trust people to work flexibly. Of course we want people to be available during core business hours, but everyone knows that if you have caring responsibilities, we'll try to accommodate that as best we can. Ultimately, we want people to do their jobs and deliver against the objectives they agree with their line manager, both in what they do and the way they do it, and that's how we'll judge their performance. We're not going to judge them on clocking in at 9 a.m. and clocking out at a certain time.

When it comes to work ethic, as the leader of the organisation, what I want to see is how our values are playing out in how an individual works and how a team works. One of the reasons we haven't set harder guidelines is because tighter boundaries can stop people having honest conversations. My view is that if you think that somebody on your team is taking the mick, sit down and have the conversation with them about why you think that. But you don't need a rigid set of rules that apply to everybody to do that.

The philosophy I have shared with our leadership team and managers is that we will not run this organisation on the lowest common denominator. We are going to run this organisation on the highest common denominator and that's how we're going to treat people. If people don't— from a work ethic, attitude, behaviour or values point of view—buy in and behave how we expect, then we face that issue and deal with it quickly. But I've been very clear we are not running this organisation and setting rules and boundaries based on the weakest link.

Marc: *What would you consider to be red flags around work ethic?*

Sally: The biggest red flag for me is untruths and people having a lazy relationship with the truth. That might mean someone jumps on a call late and says, 'I'm really sorry, my internet was down,' but you're thinking, 'OK, that's the last five times your internet's been down.' Alternatively, someone might join a call late and say, 'I'm so sorry, I completely lost track of time. I'm just late and I've got no excuse for it,' which is what I'd much rather hear.

Of course sometimes your internet does go down, or calls run over, but for me the red flag is when I'm questioning whether what the other person is saying is the truth.

MARC: *How can leaders get the best out of their people and encourage a strong work ethic, while making sure their people look after themselves?*

SALLY: That's a really great question. For some of our staff, we almost have to protect them from themselves because they're so passionate about what they do and they care so deeply. But this for me comes back to our values. One of the things we included very deliberately in our values in relation to integrity and openness was that people will be open about how they're feeling and actively take responsibility for their own health and well-being. Having that in our values statement means we can lean on that when we see people overworking. It allows us to ask the question, do you need some time off?

We can also remind them that they have to take responsibility for their own well-being, because none of us can show up and be our best selves if we're not looking after our own well-being. This idea of balance is intrinsically and philosophically connected to how we work and think, but it's also written in our behavioural statements within our values so that we can point to it and hold ourselves to it. I can say to someone, 'I see you're overworking. I'm going to help you and call it out, but you've got to take personal responsibility.'

We talk quite a lot about being a citizen of UK Sport, so I talk about the responsibility each person has as a citizen of our community, which comes with the responsibility of holding yourself and your colleagues to account on our values and behaviours.

MARC: *And what do you personally do to keep yourself in this balance?*

SALLY: I am quite fortunate, touch wood, that I don't find it that difficult to switch off, and I know in myself when I am tired and need rest. I always plan my leave before the start of each year, and I'm pretty strict with myself about taking it. But I also rely on my partner and my EA (executive assistant) Jo to help me with this. I know that when I'm tired, I am prone to mistakes and making poor decisions.

As an example, when the Whyte Review[3] was published, we received only about a month's notice that it was coming out. The publication date fell in the middle of my two-week holiday, so I cancelled my trip. I told my EA that although I'd be fine for the Whyte Review, I was tired, and I'd need her and the rest of the team to catch me in the period post-Whyte Review before I could take my rescheduled holiday. I encouraged Jo to call me out more than she normally does if she thought I was getting something wrong.

What I find interesting is that many people talk about leadership being a lonely place, and especially the CEO role being lonely, but philosophically I believe it's only lonely if you let yourself be lonely. One thing that helps me is having my own personal boardroom of people who I will go to for different things. There will be people I'll go to if I want a rant, other people I go to when I want advice and so on. I think it's incumbent on me to make sure I'm not lonely, and I feel real gratitude that I have a lot of people around me who enable me to manage myself.

MARC: *Is there anything else you'd like to add on the topic of work ethic?*

SALLY: I was brought up to believe that if you work hard, you will get results. I was the youngest of four kids, and you had to work hard to be heard. That has played really well for me throughout my entire career. I like working hard, it motivates me, and I like feeling like I've done hard graft and got a return for it. But sometimes I have to be checked on that, because not everybody who works hard does get rewarded. It isn't fair, but that's life. Some of the best athletes I've ever worked with never went to an Olympic Games, even though they worked harder than anybody else in many ways. So having a strong work ethic is not the solution to everything, which is why it's not front and centre of what I've talked about with you.

I loved talking to Sally about how work ethic is connected so closely to many other elements that are vital for high-performing teams. Here are my top three takeaways from our discussion:

1. *A strong work ethic comes from a strong set of values and clear behaviours that support those values.*

2. *To deliver high performance, you have to trust your people and expect them to behave to the highest standards, rather than create rules and guidance to fit with the lowest common denominator.*

3. *A strong work ethic is only one piece of the puzzle. It isn't a guarantee of high performance or success unless it's combined with psychological*

safety, personal responsibility, empowerment and strong values.

We've explored some excellent examples of what a strong work ethic looks like and more importantly how it contributes to a high-performing team. Whether you take inspiration from Taylor Swift, Mary Barra or Sally Munday and the team at UK Sport, it's clear there are many elements involved in creating a strong work ethic. But what if this is an area in which your team is lacking? As I said earlier, a strong work ethic is not fixed. It's not something innate which can't be developed. It's something you can work on and improve, as we've seen.

Leader as Coach

Leaders play a crucial role in fostering a strong work ethic within their teams. By setting expectations, leading by example and creating a supportive environment, they can drive productivity and engagement. Encouraging a robust work ethic helps individuals stay motivated, committed and aligned with organisational goals.

Process

Here is a 10-step guide to help you encourage a stronger work ethic in your team:

1. Define work ethic

   Articulate what a 'strong work ethic' looks like within your team. Make sure you describe both what it is AND what it isn't. You might want to replicate Sally's approach at UK Sport to create a value statement.

(continued)

(continued)

2. Align their work with organisational goals

    When employees can connect their work to the organisation's goals, they are more likely to be invested, committed and motivated to perform.

3. Co-create

    Where possible, co-create solutions with the people who will deliver them. This will strengthen the sense of ownership and engagement with the work.

4. Be an honest and open leader

    Work to gain the trust and respect of your team by being an honest and open leader. It's important to lead by example.

5. Create a sense of belonging

    Employees develop a strong work ethic when they feel they are part of the bigger picture and directly contribute to the business structure. Aligning individuals' work with organisational goals is one of the ways in which you can help create this sense of belonging.

6. Ensure effective communication

    Every month, leaders should communicate to their team about how their projects align with the organisation's current objectives, setting the tone for the collective work ethic of a team.

7. Demonstrate commitment

    Lead by example by demonstrating commitment and dedication to your work. Show up on time, meet deadlines and maintain high productivity and professionalism.

8. Model positive behaviour

   Focus on contributing to the effort without forgetting that
   people have lives outside of work. You should have one, too.

9. Say thank you

   Acknowledging and expressing gratitude for your
   employees' many contributions is essential.

10. Celebrate achievements

    Recognise and celebrate your accomplishments, both big
    and small. Acknowledging your progress reinforces positive
    behaviour and motivates everyone on your team to maintain
    a strong work ethic.

Why It Works Well

This approach strengthens a team's work ethic by fostering trust,
engagement and alignment with organisational goals. Employees
are more likely to feel valued, motivated and remain committed.

4

How Autonomy Maintains a High-Performing Team

One of the interesting points that Sally made during our conversation about work ethic was about the need for trust in any high-performing team—and a lack of trust being a red flag. When you trust your people, you can give them autonomy in how they work, which often leads to better results.

Let's face it: no one likes to be micromanaged. It creates a sense that you aren't trusted or good enough and leaves you feeling like you constantly have to justify your existence.

There are many articles citing the negative impact of micromanagement, and most of them read like the opposite of what any business is trying to achieve: low staff morale and motivation; reduced productivity and creativity; increased staff turnover; higher rates of burnout. I could go on but you get the picture.

In stark contrast to a micromanagement culture, high-performing teams work hard to give their people autonomy while creating a culture where employees feel valued, motivated and empowered to contribute their best work. This increases engagement, productivity and satisfaction, driving organisational success and growth.

However, this doesn't mean a world without any guidance whatsoever.

Let's take the world of football as an example. A high-performing football team will be clear on the game's rules and the team's strategy. Within that, the individuals are trusted to make the best decisions and take the most appropriate action at any given time. Of course, sometimes mistakes are made in the moment, but this doesn't lead to the removal of empowerment. Instead, it is accepted that things don't always go your way, and the individuals are trusted to continue to do the right thing for the team moving forward.

Businesses cease to be high-performing if their managers excessively control and monitor their employees' work. Employees feel disengaged when they are not given opportunities to take ownership of their tasks and make decisions independently. They often also become reluctant to share their ideas or take risks, leading to a lack of innovation and creativity within the organisation.

Managers should not try to solve every problem to maintain a high-performing team. Instead, they should encourage others to use their initiative and find solutions independently. This leads to efficiencies in task delivery and expedited decision-making, as employees feel their managers trust them to make crucial decisions or take on challenging work.

Be honest with yourself, do you tend to micromanage people? If so, how could you do things differently?

How to Deliver Greater Autonomy

PwC's 2024 Global Workforce Hopes and Fears Survey found that employees who feel that they can act autonomously in their day-to-day work environment tend to perform better, be more satisfied and be more committed to the organisation. Nearly half of employees would give up a 20% raise for greater control over their work.[1]

It is, therefore, no surprise that in recent years, companies across various industries have adopted unique organisational models and cultural philosophies to empower employees, foster innovation and drive growth. Notable examples include Spotify, Netflix, Google and 3M, each of which has developed a distinctive approach to autonomy and innovation within the workplace.

These companies recognise that giving employees freedom, ownership and time to explore their own ideas can yield substantial benefits, including increased productivity, more robust engagement and the development of ground-breaking products and solutions.

Spotify's 'Squad' Model

Spotify revolutionised the concept of teamwork with its innovative 'squad' model. In this structure, the company is divided into small, cross-functional teams called squads, operating almost like an independent start-up. Each squad has the autonomy to decide what projects to work on, how to approach them and how to prioritise their tasks. Within the squad model, autonomy is prioritised to foster ownership and accountability among team members.

By working independently, squad members are encouraged to experiment with new ideas and approaches without the restrictions of a top-down management structure. This model enables Spotify to adapt quickly to changing market conditions and empowers employees to take initiative and make decisions based on their expertise and understanding of the customer needs they are addressing.

This squad structure is further supported by 'chapters' and 'guilds' within Spotify, which unite individuals across squads with similar skills or interests. Chapters focus on specific technical or functional areas, allowing individuals to develop and refine their skills collaboratively. Meanwhile, guilds are informal groups that encourage knowledge sharing across the organisation.

This agile structure supports continuous improvement and collaboration, while the squads retain enough autonomy to experiment and innovate, contributing to Spotify's fast-paced development and capacity to remain competitive in the dynamic streaming industry.

Netflix's 'Freedom and Responsibility' Culture

Netflix's 'Freedom and Responsibility' corporate philosophy is a core element of its employee management and organisational structure approach. Under this philosophy, Netflix grants employees significant autonomy in achieving their goals, focusing on outcomes over rigid processes or compliance with rules.

Rather than adhering to a detailed set of policies, Netflix employees are encouraged to take ownership of their roles, think independently and make decisions that align with the company's goals. This open culture reduces bureaucratic obstacles, allowing employees to focus on driving results.

Netflix's culture is based on trusting employees to be responsible. High-performing employees are expected to manage their time and priorities effectively. This expectation of responsibility goes hand in hand with a supportive structure prioritising talent density, meaning that Netflix prioritises hiring skilled and motivated individuals. The assumption is that when competent individuals are given freedom, they are more likely to innovate and contribute meaningfully to the company's goals. This model has contributed to Netflix's ability to adapt quickly to changes in the entertainment industry.

Both Spotify and Netflix have built organisational cultures based on trust. This is a theme that will come up time and again. I loved Sally's point about creating guidelines for the highest common denominator, rather than the weakest link. Take an honest look at how you manage your team (or teams) and see how you can demonstrate greater trust in those you lead.

Google's '20% Time' Policy

Google's famous '20% time' policy is another approach that has influenced many organisations. The policy allows Google employees to dedicate 20% of their work time—roughly one day a week—to personal projects or ideas they are passionate about, even if these ideas are not directly related to their primary job responsibilities. This structured freedom is based on the belief that individuals are often most creative and productive when they can work on projects that genuinely interest them.

The 20% time policy has led to some of Google's most successful products. For example, Gmail, one of Google's most widely used services, was developed by engineer Paul Buchheit during his 20% time. Other innovations, like Google News and AdSense, were also born from this structured freedom, demonstrating the power of giving employees time to explore their ideas.

Although Google has not emphasised this policy as much in recent years, giving employees room to innovate remains integral to the company's culture. As a result of this autonomy, its employees are still driving a stream of new ideas and products that keep Google at the forefront of technology and innovation.

3M's '15% Rule'

3M, the multinational conglomerate known for its innovation in materials and consumer products, has long supported its employees' creativity through a similar policy, the '15% rule'. Under this rule, employees can spend up to 15% of their work time on personal projects, experiments or other pursuits that interest them, regardless of their relevance to immediate job duties.

This policy, which has been in place for decades, has led to the development of several iconic products, including the ubiquitous Post-it Note. The story of the Post-it Note is a classic example of how 3M's structure encourages innovation. A scientist working on a failed adhesive project found that, although what he'd created did not stick permanently, it worked perfectly for removable notes. This led to a product that revolutionised office supplies.

3M's 15% rule reflects the company's commitment to a culture of experimentation and incremental innovation. By allowing employees the time and freedom to pursue their ideas, 3M has cultivated an environment where creativity is valued and has consistently brought new products to market. This policy has positioned 3M as a leader in innovation, with thousands of patents and a reputation for encouraging employees to think outside the box.

Both Google and 3M recognise the value of allowing their employees to work on projects they're passionate about. They've found a way to give people access to this, even if it's not part of their day-to-day role. How can you start giving your employees time to develop ideas they're passionate about?

The unique approaches taken by Spotify, Netflix, Google and 3M highlight the value of autonomy and structured freedom within organisations. Each way of approaching autonomy demonstrates how giving employees ownership, flexibility and dedicated time to pursue their ideas can lead to tangible outcomes such as product innovation, enhanced employee satisfaction and overall organisational agility. By fostering an environment where employees feel trusted and supported, these companies have unlocked significant potential for creativity and innovation.

However, you'll notice that there is structure to the way in which these organisations provide autonomy. This is important because without structure, your team will fail to make meaningful progress together. This is why the defined processes, which I'll talk about in Part 2, are so important for supporting autonomy within high-performing teams.

In Conversation With Helen Webb, Chief People Officer of WHSmith

WHSmith is the UK's oldest retailer and the organisation owns a number of brands alongside that familiar high street name. InMotion, Marshall Retail Group, The Bookshop by WHSmith, Tech Express and curi.o.city are among them— and probably names you'll recognise from airports. I spoke to Helen Webb, Chief People Officer at the organisation, to learn more about how autonomy has played a key role in the company's longevity and success.

MARC: *How important is autonomy in your business?*

HELEN: I would say it's one of the building blocks of our culture. We have four values, and I think autonomy underpins each of those values. We talk about valuing the customer, valuing our people, driving for results and accountability.

Autonomy underpins each one of those, and it's also key to creating what we talk about within those values, which is entrepreneurial spirit. You can't have an entrepreneurial spirit without autonomy.

MARC: *Why is WHSmith good at giving employees autonomy?*

HELEN: We are Britain's oldest retailer and we're a UK-based PLC, so I think a lot of people might not expect us to talk about entrepreneurial spirit, but it's there. There is a lack of bureaucracy, and therefore, our people have the ability to find something new, to do something new, and shout and say, 'Hey, I'm just going to try it this way'. The most common answer they'll get when they say that is, 'Oh, that sounds fabulous. Have a go'.

This creates accountability, so that each individual is held accountable for their results. We're a very commercial business, very bottom line focused, more than any retailer I've worked in. People are held to account and that's fine if you're given the space to make decisions that can drive to answers. If you hold people to account, but you don't create the environment in which they can be accountable, then you've got a problem. If you layer that with bureaucracy, then you fail.

Nobody can be accountable under layers of bureaucracy. There's very little bureaucracy in our organisation, and very little hierarchy. If you're a buyer and you want to do something that's really interesting, more likely than not, the chief exec will find out you're doing it, come and perch on your desk and say, 'Go on then tell me. Why are we doing this? What's it going to achieve? How much profit is it going to make us?' These questions demonstrate curiosity about the new approach and they remind us what's important to the business—and therefore what we're accountable for.

MARC: *If you're someone working on the shop floor for WHSmith what does autonomy look like?*

HELEN: In a shop, we've got standard planograms [visual representations of the products in each store], but there's lots of flexibility within that. So, if you're working at InMotion in Terminal 2 at Heathrow, and our Good Vibes lines are selling really well, then you'll start promoting them. You'll start talking to customers about them. You'll ask for more stock because it's flying out. You'll have it in different places in the store, and you'll get really good at selling it. That's what autonomy looks like in one of our stores.

I've worked in food retail, where, if you haven't got a product on display at its designated place then you're in serious trouble. There's much more flexibility within what we do. We encourage our teams who are interacting with customers to take the initiative.

MARC: *How about a team that's in the back office, how does it work for your HR team?*

HELEN: If you were to think about my HR team, there's nothing stopping any of them saying, 'I've had an idea, can we try this?' We've had new people with fabulous experience from elsewhere who have come in and said, 'Can I try this 360 tool?' and the answer is 'Yep, absolutely'. 'Can I try this new provider when it comes to recruitment?' 'Yeah, no problem'. It would have to be something that was very obviously and seriously not for the benefit of the business for us to say, 'No, don't give it a try'.

MARC: *Does that freedom, that entrepreneurial spirit, play out in the senior leadership team? Does it impact how they think about strategy?*

HELEN: It absolutely does. For example, this will come into play in new market discussions. Someone might say, 'We've heard there's a tender up in this airport and I think we could actually make it work'. Budapest is a good example.

I think we are so excited by new ideas and new opportunities that, potentially, we get seduced by them. We are very commercial, but sometimes not commercial enough. It's not always easy to strike the right balance.

MARC: *If you are a person running the shop, there's a challenge around, giving people complete freedom. Do you have any advice to navigate that?*

HELEN: It's that whole old 'freedom within a framework' piece. I would say we're at the extreme end of what that framework genuinely looks like. It's not that rigid sometimes, it can be a bit floppy. But we're Britain's oldest retailer, so we must be doing something right!

MARC: *How can you spot a team that's lacking in that autonomy?*

HELEN: You can spot it in all sorts of ways. There will be noise from that team, because they can see how everyone else operates. I also think that it will come through in our engagement survey. It will also come through in the results of that team. But I don't think it's an easy culture in which to operate if you're not used to it, because that sense of autonomy can be quite scary, particularly in the really commercial teams. That drive for results, the way we hold people to account. But once someone gets used to it and embraces their autonomy, they often achieve great things.

MARC: *In some cultures, you might get blamed when you do something different and it doesn't work out. How do you manage that?*

HELEN: There are checks and balances in place, particularly in the commercial team. They won't just leave them to it with no oversight. The danger is that if somebody tries something without checking in with somebody, then that might not go so well. So, there are checks and balances in that framework. You should have at least told somebody you were about to do this. Rather than allowing people to do whatever they want, autonomy for us is more about making sure everyone knows they have the freedom to try new things and share ideas. So, we might not say yes to every idea, but everyone knows they can put things out there and that there's a good chance that they'll be allowed to run with their idea.

MARC: *Do you recruit based on this attribute?*

HELEN: Yes, particularly in the more commercial teams. We use a tool called PI, which stands for predictive index. So, we've codified the folks that really do well in our organisation, which creates a template of the temperament of the kind of person that's successful. We have had instances in the past where we've recruited from more traditional, commercial teams and then had some big failures, because people don't like the environment, don't like the culture. It is a little bit threatening because you are held to account at a relatively junior level for what you're doing. But people with an entrepreneurial spirit tend to thrive when they have autonomy coupled with strong accountability.

MARC: *What daily habits or actions can leaders use to foster greater autonomy in their teams?*

HELEN: I think it comes back to those classic HR processes: performance management and goal setting. I think you need to be clear on the goal setting, and on the framework within which you want people to operate. As a leader, I want the ideas and I'm probably going to say yes to the majority of them, but I need to know about them. Leaders need to check in regularly and ask, 'How's it going? Where are you on your goals? Last time we spoke, you said you were going to give this a go. How is it going? Let's have a look. What difference is it making? Let's have a look at stores where things have been successful. Where it's not worked, what feedback have we got?'

So I think it's about fostering real connection to the team and ongoing conversations because only then can autonomy flourish.

There's probably a misconception that autonomy means abdication, but they're two very different things. There has to be a very solid relationship between line manager and colleague if you want to create autonomy. Giving your team autonomy of action is quite different from, 'I just leave everybody alone to do their thing.'

MARC: *There's a balance between letting go and giving autonomy but maintaining control. What advice do you have for leaders who want to try to keep hold too much?*

HELEN: I think the key is reframing the conversation. If you are that type of person, then you don't just sit down and have a one-on-one with someone where you say, 'Just tell me your results and what you're doing about it.' You have more of a checklist of questions to ask, like, 'Tell me how it's going, what's working for you? What isn't working for you? What ideas are working? What isn't? What do the results say?' If you are nervous about just leaving people to it, I think you have to frame a conversation in such a way you create check-in points, but you let them do the talking. It's all about listening, more than directing.

This means you'll know what's going on and who's doing what. You'll be there to guide them if needed, but you aren't making every decision for each person on your team.

MARC: *Is there anything else that comes to mind around this topic of autonomy?*

HELEN: If you look at your Best Teams Model, you have got to have the balance in all the other areas to have autonomy. Autonomy is incredibly important for us but you can't have it without having all of those other things in place.

You have to look at goal setting, or you look at autonomy and accountability, which go hand in hand. You look at all of those attributes; autonomy can't happen in isolation. If it does happen in isolation of some of the other attributes, it can be quite destructive. For example, if you have autonomy without goal setting, recognition and psychological safety, then you're going to end up with blame culture, I suspect.

Here are my three top takeaways from my conversation with Helen:

1. *Autonomy will look different in different parts of your business, but the concept is the same— giving everyone the freedom to share new ideas and allowing them to try those new ideas as often as possible.*

2. *Strong relationships between leaders and their teams are crucial for creating autonomy, ensuring*

that you know what's going on and are able to hold people accountable in a way that drives performance.

3. *You can't have constructive autonomy without the other elements of the High-Performing Team Model in place. Accountability is particularly crucial if you want to create teams that use autonomy to drive towards high performance.*

What's clear from my discussion with Helen, and the examples I've shared in this chapter, is that there are many ways in which you can successfully give people autonomy on both a team and an individual level. But as Helen pointed out, autonomy on its own won't lead to high performance. Autonomy needs to be supported by other elements within the Best Teams Model. Giving people more autonomy is something many leaders struggle with, but what I often see is that once leaders let go of control a little bit, they don't look back.

Leader as Coach

Building a culture of autonomy and effective delegation is essential for a high-performing team. It is important that leaders prioritise their responsibilities, distribute tasks strategically and empower team members to take ownership of their work. By fostering autonomy, teams become more engaged, confident and capable of making independent decisions that align with organisational goals. Creating a culture of autonomy requires the leader to loosen their grip. The more senior you become in the organisation, the more you will have to let go.

(continued)

(continued)

Process

The following is an exercise you can use to improve autonomy and delegation within your team. If done well, this exercise will help you prioritise your responsibilities, practice effective delegation and enable your team members to take ownership of tasks.

1. Identify tasks

   The first step is for you, as the leader, to invest time understanding your priorities and responsibilities. This may seem like an onerous task, but truly understanding the depth and breadth of your responsibilities goes some way toward encouraging delegation.

   While going through this process, it is worth categorising your tasks. I like to use the Urgent-Important Matrix, or Eisenhower Matrix, as it categorises tasks into four areas based on their level of urgency and importance:

      1. Urgent and Important—I aim to get these done first.

      2. Important but Not Urgent—I schedule these.

      3. Urgent but Not Important—I delegate these.

      4. Not Urgent and Not Important—I will eliminate these.

   Completing this process will automatically generate tasks to delegate, and there may be others in areas 1 and 2 that can also be delegated.

   - Impact: It helps to remember that the point of this process is not to offload all the stuff you don't want to do, as tempting as that might be. Instead, it is about creating an environment where people can grow and succeed, and where everyone (including you) has the space to do their best work.

2. Clarify vision and goals

    Communicating the organisation's vision, mission and goals to the team reinforces how their role and responsibilities contribute to these overarching objectives.

    -   Impact: When team members see the bigger picture, they are more likely to take ownership of their work and feel motivated to make autonomous decisions that align with organisational goals.

3. Delegate responsibilities

    Delegate the tasks and responsibilities previously defined based on the team member's strengths, career goals, and readiness.

    -   Impact: This creates a culture of trust and empowerment. When leaders assign tasks thoughtfully, it encourages team members to work independently, knowing they are trusted with the responsibility.

4. Set clear expectations and boundaries

    Define what successful completion of each task looks like, including timelines, key objectives and any non-negotiable guidelines. Clearly outline any boundaries or areas where team members can exercise discretion.

    -   Impact: Clear expectations reduce confusion and increase confidence. Team members are more likely to act autonomously when they know what's expected and understand where they have the freedom to innovate.

(continued)

(continued)

5. Provide resources, tools and authority

   Ensure that team members have access to the necessary tools, resources and information. Grant them the authority to make decisions relevant to their tasks.

   - Impact: Autonomy is enhanced when employees have the tools and support to perform their roles without frequent managerial oversight. Providing authority makes it easier for team members to take ownership and act without waiting for approval.

6. Encourage decision-making and initiative

   Empower team members to make decisions within their roles. Encourage them to propose solutions, experiment and find creative approaches to their work. Reinforce that mistakes are part of learning and growth. It's also important to encourage open dialogue around these experiments, as Helen said, so that you still maintain oversight and can course-correct someone if needed.

   - Impact: This practice builds confidence and cultivates a culture of innovation. Team members become more proactive and willing to tackle challenges independently, knowing they're supported in making decisions.

7. Hold regular check-ins without micromanaging

   Schedule periodic check-ins to discuss progress, address challenges and provide guidance as needed. To avoid micromanaging, focus on results rather than monitoring every step.

   - Impact: Regular, supportive check-ins help ensure alignment and build trust. They provide a structured space for feedback without infringing on team members' autonomy.

8. Provide constructive feedback and recognise efforts

   Provide timely, constructive feedback that focuses on growth and improvement. Publicly recognise achievements and positive efforts to reinforce autonomy and accountability.

   - Impact: Positive reinforcement encourages team members to keep working autonomously, while constructive feedback provides insights for continuous improvement.

9. Reflect and adapt

   Reflect periodically on the delegation process and autonomy-building efforts. Gather feedback from team members on what helped or hindered their sense of autonomy. Adapt strategies based on what works best for the team.

   - Impact: Reflection ensures that the autonomy process remains effective and evolves as the team grows. This reinforces a culture of openness and continuous improvement.

10. Gradually increase complexity and responsibility

    As team members demonstrate capability and confidence, gradually increase the complexity and importance of the tasks they handle. Continue to provide support as needed.

    - Impact: This builds a foundation for long-term growth, enabling team members to assume leadership roles. Autonomy becomes a sustained part of team culture, leading to more capable, engaged and empowered employees.

Why It Works Well

This approach not only enhances productivity but also supports professional growth, ensuring that both leaders and team members can focus on their most valuable contributions.

5

The Role of Integrity in Maintaining High-Performing Teams

The word integrity evolved from the Latin 'integer', meaning whole or complete. When used to describe a person, it refers to the concept of living by one's values and principles. It implies trustworthiness and incorruptibility regarding a responsibility or pledge.

High-performing teams need to attract and retain people with high integrity if they are to achieve greatness. You've already heard integrity mentioned by Sally Munday in relation to creating a team with a strong work ethic, and it's an attribute that crosses over with many of the others in the Best Teams Model.

People with high levels of integrity display the qualities of being honest, ethical and morally upright in their decisions and interactions with others. Individuals with personal integrity demonstrate consistency between their words and actions, and they take responsibility for their behaviour.

Integrity is hard earned but can be quickly lost. Once lost, it can be extremely difficult, if not impossible, to recover. The worlds of business and politics are littered with people who at one point held positions of power but who failed to meet the standards expected of them by their investors, employees or voters and subsequently fell from grace. If a business employs an individual with poor integrity, you might observe that they engage in lying, cheating or deception to achieve personal gain or to cover up mistakes.

However, at least initially, there may be more subtle indicators that show they don't have the characteristic of integrity. For example, they may not lie, but they may be economical with the truth, hiding issues and shortcomings instead of facing them directly. They may also avoid taking responsibility for their actions and blame others for their mistakes or failures. It could even be as simple as having a lack of attention to detail, resulting in subpar work performance and outcomes.

High-performing teams address those with a low level of integrity at the earliest possible opportunity, occasionally through support and course correction, but more likely by letting them go altogether as they can drag a whole team down. Conversely, a team that understands the value of integrity rewards those who uphold commitments, treat others with respect and fairness and strive to do what is right, even when it may be inconvenient or unpopular.

Ask yourself these questions: Do you have people with low levels of integrity in your team? If you do, what are you going to do about them?

What Does Integrity Look Like in a High-Performing Team?

In 1978, Ben Cohen and Jerry Greenfield took a $5 correspondence course in ice cream-making from Penn State and then opened their first ice cream scoop shop in a renovated gas station in Burlington, Vermont.

The two school friends, Ben and Jerry, agreed that it was no fun being in business just to earn a living—they wanted to strike the perfect balance of joy and justice by making the world's most delicious ice cream while using the business to make the world a better place.

> 'We love making ice cream—but using our business to make the world a better place gives our work meaning'.

They do this by considering their strategy in three distinct ways:

- Thoughtful ingredients which support positive change.

- Shared success by aiming to create prosperity for everyone connected to the business.

- Making a difference by building awareness and support for activism and causes.

Ben & Jerry's has been a pioneer in advocating for social justice and environmental sustainability. The company has integrated these values into its business model, encouraging employees to engage in activism and advocacy. This commitment is not merely a marketing strategy but a core component of the company's identity. Ben & Jerry's has established partnerships with various organisations that focus on issues such as racial justice, climate change and fair-trade practices.

Their commitment to fair trade ensures that the ingredients used in their ice creams are ethically sourced, supporting farmers and communities in developing countries, for example. By openly communicating about sourcing methods and environmental impacts, Ben & Jerry's builds trust with consumers and advocates for broader systemic change in the food industry. They have also implemented initiatives to reduce their carbon footprint and promote sustainable agriculture.

But the quirky ice cream maker is far from the only business that has integrity baked into its core.

Johnson & Johnson is renowned for its 'Credo'—a set of guiding principles that places the needs and well-being of individuals above all else. This foundational document emphasises the importance of ethical behaviour and accountability, directing the company to prioritise the health and safety of consumers, employees and communities. The Credo serves as a moral compass for decision-making, influencing everything from product safety standards to employee welfare.

Johnson & Johnson's Credo has at its core the beliefs of General Robert Wood Johnson, son of the company's founder, who in 1935 wrote a pamphlet titled *Try Reality: A Discussion of Hours, Wages and the Industrial Future*.

In this pamphlet, Johnson advocated that businesses had a larger responsibility to society, which included everyone who used their products, their employees and the community.

The Credo has been revised several times since it was originally written and has often been ahead of its time:

- In 1979, wording was added to outline the company's responsibility to 'protecting the environment and natural resources'.

- In 1987, 'fathers' was added to accompany 'mothers' in the first paragraph, along with the addition: 'We must be mindful of ways to help our employees fulfill their family responsibilities'.

There is now an 8-foot-tall, 6 ton engraved quartz and limestone version of the Credo sitting in the lobby of company headquarters in New Brunswick, New Jersey.

The examples of Ben & Jerry's and Johnson & Johnson demonstrate that integrating social and environmental concerns into business models is not only beneficial for society but can also underpin long-term corporate success. A commitment to corporate social responsibility has enhanced their reputations, built trust and ultimately contributed to their success in an increasingly competitive marketplace.

You might not be in a position to make decisions about company-wide sustainability policies, but what can you do within your team to get them to start thinking about this side of business? And what can you, as a leader, do to better support the well-being of your people? Could you create your own team 'Credo' to set out what you all consider to be ethical behaviour, and use that to hold one another to account?

In Conversation With Charles Conn, Chair of Patagonia

Patagonia and its founder Yvon Chouinard had long been known for taking a sustainable approach to outdoor gear, but in 2022, the Chouinard family made the extraordinary decision to make planet Earth the company's only shareholder. In doing so, they demonstrated a new way to operate within the capitalist system. I spoke to Patagonia's Chair, Charles Conn, about how Patagonia embodies integrity to its mission of saving our home planet at every level.

MARC: *Patagonia is world-renowned for its integrity. Can you share a little bit about how that came about?*

CHARLES: My view on integrity in companies is that it usually has an origin in a person. I think in this case, that's definitely true. Integrity is doing what you say you're going to do. It's fealty to a set of values, a set of beliefs or a particular worldview. Technically, you can have integrity for an evil purpose. So I think when we're talking about integrity, we're mostly talking about commitment to something that we think is good. I think, in this case, it's very clearly Yvon Chouinard who had a very clear vision of what that could become.

It started with making better gear, and it wasn't very long before that led to an awakening in him around the potential environmental damage of outdoor activity, in particular pitons, which can scar rock. That's when he switched from pitons to climbing gear that can be removed and doesn't damage the rock.

That was the beginning of a broader set of commitments to the environment and all the creatures in it. He wasn't following someone else's lead. This was in him, in the 1950s before any of this stuff existed. He had a very clear idea about both how he thought gear should work and an emerging idea of environmentalism.

Integrity is cheap when it's easy. You're just going along with what everyone else thinks. We don't talk about integrity much then because then you're just a lemming going along with the other lemmings. I think we tend to talk about integrity when people stick to something that they feel strongly about, which, later on, turns out to be quite an important idea. So this young man who grew up as the child of Canadian immigrants to the United States in the 1950s had an idea about both a new set of athletic pursuits and the gear that would support them. And he had a set of ideas about the environment and all the creatures in it. Then, he stuck to those ideas before they were known or popular. He built something great around that. That's integrity—when no one else understands or sees the vision you have, and you stick to it anyway.

I think in most great companies that have integrity, there is a person who inoculated that company with integrity. Later on, organisations can act independently of an individual. Steve Jobs had a very clear vision, about computing and the productisation of computers, that continues after his death. It so often comes from an individual who has a vision that's different from everybody else.

MARC: *You paint a great picture of Yvon and his vision.*

CHARLES: I would say to you, Yvon Chouinard and Patagonia are one of the very few things that look better when you're close than when you're far away. The French say, 'It looks good from afar, but it's far from good'. And there's lots of stuff that's like that.

Patagonia is a place based on Yvon's personal authenticity. And he's not perfect; he's definitely got feet of clay, everybody does. But ultimately that man had a very clear idea about what the company was going to be about, and over time, an even bigger overriding purpose, which was environmentalism. He didn't start with environmentalism. He started out making the best gear. He's still, at 86 years old, thinking how I can make this better, that better, this better. That's what drives him. But there is an integrity and an authenticity in him, which is that he doesn't ever cut a corner.

Two years ago, he gave away the company. Yvon Chouinard and his family owned all the shares. They could have sold the company for six to ten billion dollars. But they gave away all the shares because Yvon believes that the environmental purpose is just so much more important. He doesn't care about being rich and doesn't have planes or boats or anything like that. He lives in the same house he has lived in for 47 years.

MARC: *How important is integrity to the business today?*

CHARLES: It's essential.

There is an important article, written in 1937 for *Economica* by Ronald Coase, called 'The Nature of the Firm'. It considers how companies exist and function. Why do they exist? Every day, people show up in return for some pay; they give their labour. But most companies are much more than that. You come with your values, you seek to find those values in your employer and your employer looks for people who share those values.

This is especially true at a company like Patagonia, which has a mission. We're in business to save our home planet. If there was a hint of cynicism, I think that would become a rot at the core of the very idea of Patagonia very quickly. I don't know how important integrity is at other businesses, but at Patagonia, it's a belief in this set of values that the company is based around. Make the best gear. Do the least harm. Use the power of business to fight for the planet. All of which lives underneath our core mission, 'We're in business to save our home planet'. Every employee knows that any of the profits of the business are given away. They support the planet.

MARC: *You've clearly laid out what integrity means for the business; how does it manifest in the individuals you employ?*

CHARLES: I can think of a thousand different ways on any given day. You can make the absolute best gear, or you can compromise a little bit. When I think about many of our competitors, they make gear that looks like it's fit for the outdoors, but really it's for urban use. At Patagonia, we'd rather the gear worked well than looked amazing. There are thousands of little choices we make every day at Patagonia that mean we don't compromise on the functional use of our gear.

You could pick the easy path. You can sell the easy stuff, or you can do the hard work and find a way to make a raincoat that works but doesn't use dangerous chemicals and doesn't use hydrocarbon-based fuels. That sometimes means it isn't the most beautiful thing, although William Morris said it was OK to look for beauty after you had functionality sorted. It's often not the most profitable thing. It's not the easy thing. It's the hard thing. Integrity is those choices.

There are pictures of Yvon with Rick Ridgeway from the early days when they were trying to figure out what would keep you warm when it was wet. And as you know, wool can do that to a certain extent. Down is terrible when it gets wet. Cotton's really rotten. And these guys found this furry industrial fleece fabric; then, they shaved a spot for the pocket. It looks silly, but now it's copied by couture brands everywhere, the shaved place for the pocket! That's classic Patagonia to me.

MARC: *You've shared the upside of integrity for the business and for the planet, are there any impacts on the people within the organisation that you have to be aware of?*

CHARLES: If your integrity is to a mission that no longer has relevance in the world—perhaps you were a buggy whip manufacturer after the invention of automobiles—that can be a suicide mission.

When Claire, Yvon's daughter, wrote the charter for the Patagonia Purpose Trust, the charitable institution that now owns the shares for the company, she said: 'We are fundamentally committed to our mission. If that is a suicide mission, so be it'. They would rather have the company cease to exist than to compromise on what they're about. The mission of the company now is very simple; we're in business to save our home planet and anything that doesn't contribute to that, we don't want to be part of. They would rather cease to exist and have made a point about capitalism, a negative point about capitalism. If that isn't integrity, I don't know what is.

That's a heavy burden. If you're an employee in a place like Patagonia, and you're not living up to that, the pain of it is so much greater. Imagine working for Pepsi, and your share of sugary drinks drops by 1%, OK, it affects profitability. People may lose their jobs, but when you go home at night, do you lay in bed thinking, 'Oh my God, we've lost some of our share of sugary drinks?' No, you do not.

At Patagonia, you'll never go to bed and say, 'We've saved our home planet'. You go to bed and think 'Shit, have we done anything at all to save our home planet?' So I think it's hard to see the impact. It's easier to see that you're not making an impact. This kind of integrity to a mission has an enormous price.

High praise from Yvon would be, 'That's good, we can do better'. That's the attitude of a place like this, and that's challenging to live every day. These are not easy places. People have this idea that working for mission-driven organisations where there's integrity to a mission is fun and easy. No. It's the hardest thing.

MARC: *When you know how tough that's going to be for people coming into the business, how do you assess them?*

CHARLES: There's nothing more important than hiring people who are both technically talented and deeply committed. It's not an easy thing to do. A lot of times Yvon will go climbing or fishing with someone to get to really know people before you put them in the most important positions. When I was running my start-up company, we'd always go and play Frisbee golf with people. You learn so much from people doing a round of Frisbee golf, compared to sitting in a room saying, 'Right, tell me what your shortcomings are...' 'Oh, I work too hard'.

As you know in your work, the wrong people are just so deadly for mission-driven organisations. It takes so long to hire somebody, and it takes a considerable amount of time to figure out you made a mistake. Then, it takes a considerable amount of time to get rid of them, and then you're right back at the beginning.

MARC: *Do you coach and mentor them?*

CHARLES: Yvon, still to this day, goes and meets everybody, and we have a Patagonia University, where people learn our values. You can't just expect people to get it osmotically. It would be easy to say, 'We're in business to save our home planet. Let's all put on some tie-dye and go to the beach'. But that's not how we work. Yvon is all about quality all the time. The only thing that really works is seeing something that needs to be better, prototyping something that makes it better, then taking it into the field, breaking it and then building it again. That's the core of Patagonia.

MARC: *You mentioned earlier that integrity can be centred on a bad thing; where do you think modern businesses are at the moment? Do you think there's a need to focus more on positive integrity?*

CHARLES: If you look at the most reputable businesses in the United States, Patagonia is always in the top five and recently in the top one. But in that same group are businesses like Chick-fil-A. It is a business that makes fried chicken sandwiches. They're also famous for their anti-LGBTQ stance. And one of the reasons people like Chick-fil-A is not just because the chicken sandwiches are good, but because some people like that mission, they like the anti-LGBTQ approach. They have integrity for what they are. They know what they're about, and their customers are good with that, whatever the rest of us think about that.

So I don't think you need to look at terrible political movements to see that there is such a thing as integrity in wrong things, but I think it's so much better if we can look at any kind of organisation and think, 'This is making our lives better, and maybe even more importantly, the lives of future generations, not only of humans, but other creatures too'. It's easier to sign up for something that feels like it's progressing humankind as a species. I think that's better than a fried chicken sandwich and some shitty HR policies.

MARC: *Is there a lesson you think leaders should take from your experience?*

CHARLES: Maybe it's implicit in everything we've said already, but like all values and virtues, integrity only matters if it's actually *practiced*. You can say you believe in grace, or you believe in kindness but it doesn't matter at all if you don't actually put that into practice in the biggest and smallest ways. You have to actually live integrity.

Practice is a thing you think of with a great musician or a great artist, a great athlete, or when you think about craftsmen. I think there's something lovely about practice, especially when it's in all the little things because I think hypocrisy is just around the corner if you don't.

Having this conversation is like practice. It's a reminder. Because every day you can take the easy route or you can take the hard route. Let's pick the hard route.

I very much enjoyed practicing with Charles. Here are my three top takeaways from our conversation:

1. *Integrity starts with a clear mission and vision that other people can get behind and align themselves with.*

2. *Often integrity requires us to take the difficult path or make difficult choices. When we have integrity, we willingly take the hard route because we know that we are making a positive impact on the world and those around us in doing so.*

3. *Daily practice leads to integrity, both in business and in life. As Charles said, we can only have integrity if we practice it in the big and small things every day. We have to keep asking ourselves how we can show integrity for our mission, and then do that.*

One of the things that really stuck with me from my conversation with Charles is the idea that integrity is a daily practice. When you look at any of the examples of high-performing teams in this chapter, or indeed this book, you can see that the actions they take are consistent. Achieving high performance doesn't mean having appealing values stuck on a wall. It means living those values, and making choices that align with those values, every minute of every day and at every level of an organisation.

As Charles also pointed out, it is essential to hire people with integrity into your organisation, but that isn't always easy to spot in traditional interview processes.

Leader as Coach

A person's morals and integrity develop over a lifetime, starting in early childhood and evolving through experiences and reflection. In their early years, children learn basic right and wrong from caregivers, and by school age, they begin to understand social expectations, empathy and fairness. Adolescents then explore personal identity and start solidifying their values, often influenced by peers.

Life experiences, education and exposure to different perspectives in early adulthood deepen their ethical beliefs, making integrity a conscious choice. Even in later life, morals

(continued)

(continued)

and integrity continue to evolve through self-reflection, challenges and changing worldviews shaped by each person's values and choices.

It's clear that as a leader, you can have a positive impact on an individual and your team's integrity. Being trustworthy and admitting your mistakes, talking openly and honestly, and standing by your beliefs will influence the behaviour of others—as it has with Yvon Chouinard. However, it is important to recruit people into your team who have integrity.

Process

Not everyone can take prospective candidates climbing, fishing or for a game of frisbee, so here are some insightful interview questions to assess a candidate's personal integrity and ethical values. These questions aim to reveal how they approach ethical dilemmas, maintain trust and uphold personal accountability. Conversations with candidates based on the following or other similar questions will help you determine if a candidate has the levels of integrity you expect within your high-performing team.

1. **Describe a time when you had to make a difficult ethical decision. How did you approach it, and what was the outcome?**

   ○ *Purpose*: To see how they handle complex ethical situations and whether they prioritise integrity.

2. **Have you ever witnessed a coworker doing something against company policy or ethical standards? What did you do?**

   ○ *Purpose*: To gauge their willingness to take action when encountering unethical behaviour.

3. **How do you define personal integrity, and why is it important in a professional setting?**

    ○ *Purpose*: To understand their views on integrity and its role in their work.

4. **Tell me about a time when you made a mistake. How did you handle it?**

    ○ *Purpose*: To assess their honesty and accountability in admitting and addressing errors.

5. **Have you ever been asked to do something at work that you felt was morally questionable? How did you respond?**

    ○ *Purpose*: To evaluate how they navigate situations where their values might conflict with directives.

6. **How do you ensure transparency and honesty when communicating with others, especially when delivering difficult news?**

    ○ *Purpose:* To see if they prioritise honesty and clear communication, even in challenging situations.

7. **Describe a time when you had to stand up for what you believed was right, even if it wasn't popular.**

    ○ *Purpose*: To understand their courage and commitment to doing what's right.

8. **How do you handle situations where you disagree with a supervisor's or leader's actions or decisions?**

    ○ *Purpose*: To see if they can respectfully address ethical conflicts with authority figures.

(continued)

(continued)

9. **How would your previous coworkers describe your integrity and honesty?**

   ○ *Purpose*: To prompt self-reflection and provide insight into their reputation for integrity among peers.

Why It Works

These questions help determine someone's integrity by assessing their past behaviour, decision-making process and personal values in ethical situations. By evaluating how someone has handled ethical challenges in the past, these questions go beyond theoretical knowledge and provide real insights into their character, ensuring that they align with an organisation's values and ethical expectations.

6

How a Growth Mindset Maintains High-Performing Teams

No one should ever consider themselves the 'finished article'. If you think you are at the pinnacle and there is nothing more you can learn, then you are probably not in a high-performing team. Even the greatest Olympian of all time, Michael Phelps, winner of 23 Gold medals, had a coach who constantly worked with him as he aimed to be stronger, fitter and faster.

Warren Buffett, one of the world's most successful business investors, dedicates 80% of his day to reading. As he says, 'Read 500 pages . . . every day. That's how knowledge works. It builds up, like compound interest. All of you can do it, but I guarantee not many of you will do it'.[1]

Both Phelps and Buffett epitomise what it is to have a growth mindset. When the people within a business have a growth mindset, they demonstrate a commitment to develop both themselves and others, as they create an environment where learning is valued, supported and integrated into everyday practices.

Maintaining and encouraging a curious mind helps a high-performing team identify trends, innovate more effectively and grow the organisation, thereby driving long-term success and competitiveness.

If the people within a business lack a growth mindset, it may remain static in its processes, products or services without evolving to meet changing market demands or technological advancements. Employees may resist adopting new technologies, methods or practices. Without ongoing training and skill development, there may be a risk of them becoming stagnant in their roles, leading to decreased morale and engagement.

High-performing teams accept that they operate within a competitive landscape where many things are out of their control. However, maintaining a growth mindset is not one of them and a focus on it can drive a team forward. It is a mindset where every situation, both successes and failures, is perceived as a learning opportunity.

Take time to reflect now, when was the last time you proactively looked to learn? NOW is the answer! But how about your team? Do they have a growth mindset?

Understanding the Growth Mindset

The concept of the growth mindset was developed by psychologist Carol Dweck in the late 20th century. Dweck's research focused on understanding how people perceive their abilities and intelligence. Through her studies, she identified two primary mindsets: fixed and growth.

A fixed mindset is the belief that intelligence and abilities are static and unchangeable. Conversely, a growth mindset is the belief that these traits can be developed through effort, learning and perseverance. Dweck's seminal book, *Mindset: The New Psychology of Success*, published in 2007, brought these ideas to a broader audience.[2]

Dweck's work demonstrated that individuals with a growth mindset are more likely to embrace challenges, persist in the face of setbacks and view effort as a path to mastery. Her research has significantly impacted education, parenting and organisational leadership, promoting the idea that fostering a growth mindset can lead to greater achievement and personal development.

The antithesis of a growth mindset is a fixed one and the world of business is littered with examples of what can happen when your company has a fixed mindset. Blockbuster's failure to adapt to the changing entertainment industry is one of the best examples of how a fixed mindset can lead to a business' downfall.

Blockbuster's brick-and-mortar model was successful for a time. It started out as a video rental store in the 1980s, progressing to DVD and video game rentals in the 1990s. Although the chain adapted to different formats for delivering media, its fundamental business model didn't shift. Blockbuster's fixed mindset was 'if it ain't broke, don't fix it' and it eventually brought them down.

In 1997, the year that Netflix was founded, one of Blockbuster's core income streams was its late fee charge of $1 a day. It was extremely lucrative bringing in $800 million a year.

When developing his value proposition, Netflix co-founder Reed Hastings used to share a story about a $40 late fee he had accumulated at Blockbuster and how this inspired him to create Netflix. It was a story that had a pinch of Hollywood about it but it did make a point. Netflix was going to compete with Blockbuster and offer a flat monthly rate for DVDs delivered directly to customers' homes, without late fees.

In 2000, Netflix and its co-founder Marc Randolph offered to sell Blockbuster a 49% stake in their company for $50 million. However, Blockbuster's then-CEO John Antioco rejected the offer. Blockbuster filed for Chapter 11 bankruptcy protection in 2010. By contrast, in 2023, Netflix was worth $150 billion.

A Growth Mindset Across Disciplines

Leonardo da Vinci, born on 15 April 1452, was more than an incredibly gifted artist. He possessed a boundless curiosity and an insatiable thirst for knowledge that drove him to master a vast array of subjects. While widely celebrated as one of the most influential painters of all time, his interests spanned far beyond the arts, covering areas as diverse as science, mathematics, anatomy, geology and even engineering.

His interdisciplinary brilliance marked him as the quintessential 'Renaissance man', a title that reflects not only his breadth of skill but his mindset of constant exploration and innovation. Leonardo's scientific pursuits were years ahead of his time, with anatomical studies that offered detailed insights into the human body, sketches of flying machines and engineering blueprints that laid the groundwork for inventions centuries later.

Among Leonardo's more notable inventions were his designs for an ornithopter, inspired by the structure and movement of birds' wings, and a precursor to the modern helicopter. These designs demonstrated his understanding of mechanics and aerodynamics at a time when the concept of flight for humans was still unimaginable. He filled his journals with observations and intricate drawings, crossing fields and forming a comprehensive worldview of interconnected knowledge.

His investigations into light, for example, informed his understanding of painting, while his studies in anatomy enriched his representations of the human form in works like Vitruvian Man and The Last Supper. This synthesis of art and science exemplifies what it means to be a polymath— someone with profound understanding across multiple disciplines.

Many historical figures have shared his drive for interdisciplinary exploration, including Aristotle, who delved into philosophy, biology and physics; Galileo Galilei, who contributed to astronomy, physics, and engineering; and Marie Curie, who pioneered research in physics and chemistry. Each of these individuals exemplified a holistic approach to knowledge, refusing to confine themselves to a single field. Thomas Jefferson's contributions to architecture, literature and politics and Albert Einstein's integration of philosophy into his work on theoretical physics further underscore how intellectual diversity can spark monumental achievements.

One critical takeaway from Leonardo's life and accomplishments is the importance of allowing individuals the freedom to explore multiple interests. By avoiding narrow definitions of expertise and instead fostering a space for interdisciplinary growth, organisations can cultivate more well-rounded, innovative thinkers.

Take a moment to think about how you can give those on your team a bit more freedom in what they learn and experiment with. Could you set aside time each week or month where employees can explore their own interests, much like 3M and Google do? Or maybe you could encourage members of your team to come together and share what they're passionate about outside of work, educating and strengthening team bonds in the process?

From Growth Mindset to Innovation

This openness to diverse skills is especially relevant in modern workplaces, where cross-functional knowledge and creativity are often the driving forces behind successful innovation. For instance, Steve Jobs, co-founder of Apple, held a similarly broad range of interests, from technology to calligraphy and dance. Jobs' varied passions allowed him to bridge the gap between art and technology, creating Apple products that were not only functional but also aesthetically groundbreaking. His understanding of beauty and design—rooted in his artistic inclinations—was instrumental in creating devices like the iPhone, which combined technological innovation with user-friendly design and reshaped the tech industry.

Several forward-thinking companies today encourage this polymathic mindset by investing in their employees' continuous development and fostering an environment that values creativity and cross-disciplinary exploration.

Adobe, for example, has implemented programs like the 'Learning Fund', which reimburses employees for educational expenses, supporting their pursuit of knowledge outside their immediate job roles. Additionally, Adobe's

'Kickbox' initiative provides employees with resources and funding to explore new ideas, promoting a culture of risk-taking and innovation. By supporting employee-driven projects and allowing room for experimentation, Adobe exemplifies how companies can benefit from encouraging a growth mindset. Employees who are empowered to pursue their interests and learn from their mistakes are more likely to bring fresh perspectives and innovative solutions to the table.

Pixar, another creative industry leader, cultivates a growth mindset by fostering an environment of feedback, creativity, and collaboration. Pixar's 'Braintrust meetings' are an example of constructive, open feedback sessions where employees review projects without hierarchy, focusing on improvement and creative exchange. This approach has helped Pixar maintain a high standard of storytelling and animation quality, as employees are encouraged to experiment, make mistakes and learn continuously. The company's commitment to creative freedom and collaborative learning has enabled it to produce a long list of critically acclaimed and beloved films.

Salesforce also encourages its employees to adopt a growth mindset, primarily through its 'Trailhead' learning platform. This platform provides resources for developing new skills, allowing employees to set ambitious goals, seek feedback and learn from their experiences. By creating an accessible learning environment, Salesforce cultivates a culture of continuous improvement, making it possible for employees to grow in areas beyond their immediate job requirements.

Similarly, LinkedIn promotes a growth mindset through initiatives like 'InDay', which gives employees a day each month to focus on personal growth, community service or innovation. This time is an opportunity for employees to explore new challenges, engage with causes they are passionate about and build skills through LinkedIn Learning. By prioritising personal and professional development, LinkedIn demonstrates its commitment to an adaptable, evolving workforce.

The Renaissance ideals of holistic learning and intellectual curiosity continue to shape our understanding of what it means to be a well-rounded, impactful contributor in any field. Embracing this spirit of polymathy can enable both individuals and organisations to achieve new levels of excellence and innovation.

Creativity and innovation requires space, so take a moment to think about how you can create that space for those on your teams. Simon Lambert offers some excellent advice in our conversation. But perhaps you can follow the lead of Adobe or LinkedIn by providing the means and time for people to learn something new and experiment? Or could you introduce a forum like Pixar's 'Braintrust meetings' to encourage everyone on your team to freely share their thoughts and input on initiatives? One thing that is clear from all of these examples is that, as with many of the attributes we're covering, there is no single 'right' way to go about this.

In Conversation With Simon Lambert, Microsoft UK Chief Learning Officer

Microsoft is renowned for the work it has done to embed the concept of having a growth mindset within its company culture. I spoke to Simon Lambert, the UK business' Chief

Learning Officer, to find out more about how they've done it, and what lessons teams and organisations of all sizes can learn from their journey.

MARC: *Satya Nadella, Microsoft's CEO, has been a vocal advocate of the growth mindset. I'm interested to hear your thoughts on why it's considered to be so important for your business?*

SIMON: Well, I think if you go all the way back to 2014, which is when Satya took over as CEO, he was asking some really big questions of the company. What does Microsoft stand for? If Microsoft no longer existed in the world, what gap would it leave? These were really big, strategic, meaningful, purposeful questions. Off the back of that, he established a new Microsoft mission, 'Empowering every person and organization on the planet to achieve more'. So that was what we were anchoring on.

He chose the words very carefully in that mission statement, 'Empowering every person and organization on the planet', because we had a massive scale. But he recognised that to get there, we needed to change the organisation and the way in which the organisation operated. Satya subscribed to Carol Dweck's approach around growth mindset, because he believed that. He very famously said that Microsoft needed to move from being an organisation of know-it-alls, to an organisation of learn-it-alls. The way to get there was to embrace this idea of innate curiosity, and accept that not everything is defined. Things can be learned. Things can be trained. And everyone has the opportunity if they apply themselves in the right way.

People talk about fixed mindset versus growth mindset, and Satya made it very clear that this wasn't about seeking out fixed mindset people in the organisation, because everybody switches between having a growth mindset and a fixed mindset at various different times. The challenge was to identify yourself when you're falling into that trap [of a fixed mindset] and say, 'Okay, how can I move out of this fixed mindset, think differently and have a growth mindset?'

By making this the focus, we were able to create a culture of experimentation; a culture where people feel like they can get things wrong; a culture where risk is managed, but managed in an innovative way; and a culture where we can still really push the edges around innovation and technology. This anchored the culture in terms of how we wanted to bring to life this new mission.

MARC: *Can I just jump back to one thing you said there, which was about spotting where people are as they sway from fixed to growth mindset. What are you looking for?*

SIMON: First of all, we had to get everyone to understand what that concept was. That involved a complete company-wide series of workshops done in every market around the world, and across every single business, to really talk about what a growth mindset means, because it means different things to different people. Ultimately, we wanted the conversation to be about how we could encourage and develop that.

That involved an awful lot of engaging top down, bottom up, mid management and following the change management process I'm sure you're familiar with to drive this shift, but at its core it started with level setting. What does a growth mindset and a fixed mindset mean for everyone? We wanted everyone to be clear on the fact that you can switch between the two, and that's okay. You've just got to catch yourself [when you're in a fixed mindset].

One of the things we did as an organisation, which I think is probably one of the things that had the most success, was changing how we recognise and reward people for performance. Previously that recognition and reward was driven off how well you achieved against a set of key performance indicators (KPIs). When we started this focus on a growth mindset, there was a real push to say, 'Look, that's important, but it's not the only thing that's important'. As a result, we now have three ways in which we recognise and reward performance.

The first is: are you performing against your key KPIs? Because that's still an important component of it. The second component, which was new, is how are you helping others grow? And the third one, which was also new, is how are you taking the work of others and leveraging it? So, if you think about those three concentric circles coming together like a Venn diagram, with the sweet spot being in the middle, everybody—every manager, every review, all the way up to Satya—has to come to the table to say, 'I've hit my targets. Here's how I've helped others grow across the company, connected others and really brought the world together. And finally, here's how I've taken the work from other people and really built on it'.

That was, I think, one of the biggest things that impacted on the cultural change, because it was inherently tied to performance. It was tied to remuneration. It was tied to your bonus, and your salary. I guess it forced it to some degree, but more importantly it brought it to life. It made it real. It sent a clear signal that we are going to recognise you when you take somebody else's work, recognise it's good and build on it, as opposed to dismantling it, which can happen in corporate cultures.

MARC: *What did you do as an organisation to focus people on this change, because being told you're going to be reviewed like that doesn't mean you keep it front of mind?*

SIMON: It's obviously the big things, as I've described, but it's also the small things. It was helping people see it's not just about what you do, but about how you do it. How are you bringing people along with you on the journey? How are you collaborating with others? There was a whole series of leadership training that everybody went through, and still goes through.

We still obviously celebrate work, even when it's clearly not gone quite to plan by the way, and that's really important. We focus on celebrating learning as much as acknowledging successes. This behaviour has been driven by the leadership. We had a big project that didn't go very well. It was very public. Satya effectively said, 'Thanks for trying. We didn't quite get it right, but now go away, learn from it and do it again'. Responding to it in this way sent the message across the organisation that it's okay to not get it quite right, even if it's a big project, as long as we learn from it, recognise it and come back differently.

That's a big example but it's also evident in the micro behaviours that you see. We had to bring this concept to life, day in and day out. It would have been very easy for people to weaponise it and say, 'That's not very growth mindset', because a manager doesn't like hearing somebody challenge them. But people have got over that, and actually challenging something is a growth mindset in itself.

In essence, the behaviours of the leadership team all the way down the management chain have really brought the growth mindset concept to life and we shine a light on those moments as much as we can, to demonstrate that this isn't just a once and done activity. This is a new way to operate.

MARC: *I'm interested in what you're saying there about how, as with any good thing, it can sometimes be used against you. What other challenges have you had trying to get people to absorb this as a way of being within Microsoft?*

SIMON: Like anything it's a behavioural change. And that means it's all about habits.

People were also invited to decide whether they were committed to the new mission and culture or not because this was the direction in which the company was going. We gave people a chance to sign up to this, or to make a different choice with a different organisation, which was hard for some people, but nonetheless an important component. There was a massive change in how the organisation started to measure its success.

There was a massive change operationally in how we built new processes into the business. It was a very strong signal we were leaving that old regime behind, and moving into a new regime. That shift doesn't mean we don't review the business, and it doesn't mean we don't do all the stuff you'd expect. But there was a recognition that the company needed to do things differently. And that made people think, this is really happening.

MARC: *I always think culture change is like turning a supertanker but you have the opportunity with new people coming into the business to clearly define what is expected of them. Did you start looking for a different kind of person to come into the business?*

SIMON: It's fair to say that now when a manager is looking to bring somebody into the business, one of the aspects they're looking at is, 'Can this person demonstrate an innate curiosity, which could potentially point to a growth mindset?' We obviously look at core values like Diversity & Inclusion, customer obsession and all that kind of goodness, but the interviewer will screen candidates based on their ability to demonstrate how they've been able to address a challenge in the past and think differently about it. Or whether they can bring to life an example where they've taken feedback that something isn't working, and how they responded to that. Whenever we're recruiting, we're asking ourselves, 'Can this person demonstrate that they have a learn-it-all, curious nature that will ultimately support this idea of a growth mindset?'

MARC: *What advice should we be putting out there for anyone who wants to try and help their team have a better growth mindset?*

SIMON: You have to have a culture of learning. You have to have a culture where people feel like they've got the time, permission and space to learn. If you speak to any Learning & Development professional, across any business, typically the number one challenge from employees is 'I don't have enough time'. So when you're trying to encourage people to think creatively, to solve a problem, or encourage people to maybe learn something new, or get them to be curious about something that they haven't previously been curious about, you need to have a culture that allows that. This means building a culture of learning. We have invested significantly in creating a culture of learning, and the way we bring that to life is by making time and space.

For example, we use things like learning days, learning weeks or learning months, where we send a signal across the organisation that we want the focus to be on learning. To be honest, they're the antithesis of what we need, because we don't want people just to learn on one day or one week. We want them to learn all the time. But the point we're making is that this is so important to the organisation and the company that we're going to carve out time and give each individual an opportunity to learn over this day, this week or this month.

We also have a process called Connects, which are twice yearly performance reviews where the manager talks to their individual team members. As part of this process, the individual is required to reflect on something that didn't quite go right, and how they would do it differently, or how they would reflect on that in the future. Again, this isn't about judging, or saying that it was a disaster.

This is about saying, 'Okay, that didn't quite work. What did you learn from it? How would you do it differently?'

If you think about creating this culture of learning in terms of behaviour, we encourage leaders right the way up to our CEO to demonstrate that they're always learning and always curious. This could be something simple, like saying, 'I've read a new book, and it's great. Here are the three things I took out of it'. Or it could be starting a team meeting by asking if anyone has got anything that they've learned recently that they think would benefit the rest of the team. Or even just taking the time to invite people to present when they've had a bit of a challenge and explain how they've responded to it.

In doing so, we bring to life the impact this is having on helping to solve customers' and partners' challenges—to help them achieve their goals. At this point, the individual with the challenge can demonstrate that they're prioritising customer obsession and show the impact that's having.

Here are my three top takeaways from my conversation with Simon:

1. *None of us have a purely growth mindset or purely fixed mindset. We switch between the two—the opportunity lies in noticing when we're in a fixed mindset and finding a way to transition ourselves back to a growth mindset.*

2. *Creating a culture focused on learning is essential to encourage open and honest discussions of failures as well as successes. Building this into performance reviews makes it real for employees.*

3. *To embed learning in your organisation's culture, you have to make time and space for it. This shows everyone that you value learning, creativity, innovation and experimentation.*

To create a growth mindset environment, businesses must provide resources and opportunities for ongoing skill development, allow employees to take risks, try new ideas, learn from failures and create an environment where constructive feedback is valued and used for growth—as we've seen from the various examples in this chapter.

If you've never thought about learning within the workplace in this way, it can be a significant cultural shift. But as Simon and Microsoft show, when you dedicate time and energy to cultivating a growth mindset at every level of an organisation, it has significant positive impacts. The point is that you have to start somewhere, and doing this kind of work as a group in the early days is often easier than doing it on your own. An exercise like the one that follows can also provide a template that people can use individually to assess situations that don't go to plan, and learn from them.

Leader as Coach

I personally feel as though I have learnt more from my failures than my successes. Take the 'failure' of winning a Silver medal in Atlanta. After a period of self-reflection, it drove me on to improve numerous things in my preparation and interactions with the British Swimming Team, most importantly was that I needed to better listen to my teammates.

(continued)

(continued)

A group reflection exercise can lead to both individuals and the team as a whole learning from a failure. The purpose is to reframe setbacks as learning opportunities, and it also provides the leader with an opportunity to role model why a growth mindset is so important.

Process

Identify a team failure:

As a team, discuss a recent project or task where the outcome didn't meet expectations. Choose a specific example everyone can relate to.

Analyse together:

Reflect on what contributed to the setback. It is crucial that everyone, regardless of role, gets involved here to ensure nothing is missed and equally as important is that this doesn't turn into a blame game. Few things will inhibit growth more than blame.

Identify learnings:

For each contributing factor, discuss what the team learned. Consider insights about personal contributions, team dynamics or process adjustments.

Develop a team improvement plan:

Collaboratively, outline steps to improve. Define specific actions the team will take in future projects to help prevent a similar outcome and who will own those actions.

Refine:

Getting a perspective from outside the team can enhance your plan. Share your reflections and plan with another team or a mentor for external feedback.

Implement and monitor:

Apply the plan in your next project, assigning roles to monitor progress and check in regularly as a team. Make adjustments based on ongoing observations and feedback.

Make it routine:

Practice doesn't make perfect. Perfect practice makes perfect. Repeat this reflection process regularly.

Why It Works

These steps shift the team's focus from fixed outcomes, 'we failed', to evolving processes, 'we are improving'. They emphasise that challenges and setbacks are not dead ends but part of the process towards success, reinforcing the belief that skills and performance improve through effort and reflection.

Empowering People for High Performance

Empowered people are essential in any high-performing team. You can have the most advanced tech or best product in the world, but without a team of people with a strong work ethic, who have integrity and autonomy, and who want to learn and grow, your business won't go far.

In fact, your business won't even get off the ground. This is why those who lead high-performing teams focus on attracting and retaining people with a strong work ethic, integrity and who demonstrate the traits of a growth mindset. Once they have hired these people, they empower them by giving them autonomy in their work.

Leaders of truly high-performing teams don't leave any of these attributes to chance. They actively engage with their people to ensure that all four of these attributes are maintained and actively work to improve any that appear to be sliding. You've heard from some incredible leaders in these chapters, and although their organisations and backgrounds may be very different, the one thing they all have in common is the way in which they take very intentional steps to empower their people.

That's what the exercises I've shared in each chapter are designed to do—use these within your own team to take control of each of these attributes and embed them firmly in your culture. This is not a process you just do once. It's an ongoing leadership practice that will support your team and organisation to reach ever greater heights. As Charles Conn said, it's a practice and one that you never finish.

Part II

Defined Processes

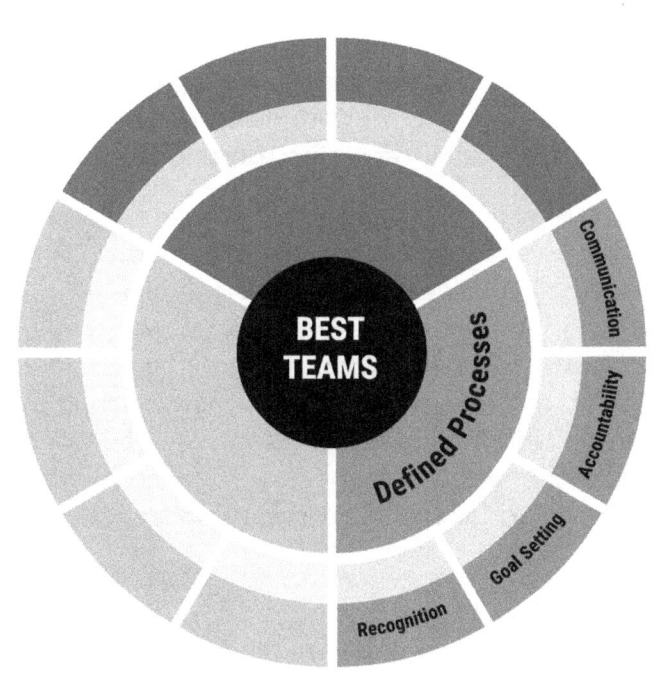

In 1961, President John F. Kennedy challenged NASA to land a man on the Moon and return him safely to Earth before the decade's end. This ambitious goal became the Apollo Program. Achieving it required solving complex scientific, engineering and logistical challenges. NASA also had to coordinate over 400,000 people, from engineers and scientists to contractors and administrators, working across multiple facilities.

This is why, when I was considering examples of how defined processes enable teams, this stood out.

NASA implemented a rigorous system of meticulously developed processes to govern every aspect of the Apollo Program. This system ensured consistency, safety, quality, accountability and collaboration among thousands of individuals and organisations. This structured approach was critical to managing the complexity of landing humans on the Moon and safely returning them to Earth.

Recognising each team member's expertise and contribution was essential to the success of the Apollo Program. By defining clear roles within systems engineering, NASA ensured that all specialists from various disciplines could work cohesively. The communication channels established across the thousands of team members allowed for seamless collaboration, ensuring that each component—from spacecraft to support systems—was compatible and reliable, thus supporting the program's overarching goal.

Detailed objectives were set at every stage of the mission. This included rigorous testing and quality assurance protocols to simulate different scenarios and identify potential points of failure. Each piece of hardware underwent exhaustive trials, ensuring readiness for deployment and reducing risks during critical mission phases.

Accountability was woven into the fabric of NASA's approach. Project management systems created clear timelines, milestones and robust risk management strategies, ensuring that the program remained on track. Teams were accountable for meeting deadlines, addressing challenges and maintaining efficiency throughout the complex process, all of which kept the Apollo missions on schedule despite their magnitude.

Communication played a key role in preparing astronauts and mission controllers for the realities of space exploration. Through extensive training and simulation, teams rehearsed a wide range of potential scenarios, fostering confidence and reducing human error during high-stakes phases. Furthermore, NASA promoted iterative improvement by consistently learning from past experiences. After the tragic Apollo 1 fire, the organisation incorporated the lessons learned into future missions, improving safety protocols and procedures to ensure the continued success of the program.

On 20 July 1969, the Apollo 11 mission successfully landed Neil Armstrong and Buzz Aldrin on the Moon, while Michael Collins orbited above in the command module. This success was a technological triumph and a testament to the power of well-defined and rigorously implemented processes. The Apollo Program continued to deliver six successful Moon landings, solidifying its legacy as one of history's greatest team accomplishments.

The Apollo Program highlights how NASA turned an ambitious vision into reality by establishing clear roles, consistent workflows and rigorous quality controls.

Empowered people need processes and systems that support them—as we can see from the NASA example, and as we heard from Sally, Helen, Charles and Simon in the previous chapters. As you move through these chapters around the attributes associated with defined processes, you'll find conversations with leaders whose teams and organisations have mastered creating processes that support creativity, innovation and high performance. I invite you to take their knowledge and consider how you might apply some of it within the team or teams you lead.

7

How Communication Impacts High-Performing Teams

Once you have the foundation of empowered people in order, you can move on to the processes required to create a platform on which they can be brilliant. One of the key skills that all high-performing teams do well is communication.

Today there are about 6,900 known living languages. That presents plenty of potential for communication problems. But you don't need to be talking to someone who speaks a different language to run into problems. Communicating clearly and meaningfully with people who speak the same language can be just as difficult.

The good news is that there have never been more means of communicating with your team, stakeholders, or customers, which makes it easier to find the best channel to use to communicate your message or discuss challenges and opportunities.

You might choose to put pen to paper or type an email. Perhaps you will use a tool like WhatsApp, MS Teams, Skype,

Discord, Zoom, Slack, or Google Meet; a social network such as Facebook, or Instagram; or a project management tool like ClickUp.

You could even speak face to face with someone, but you still have to remember to listen and listen at the right level! There are three levels to listening:

- Level one is listening primarily to yourself, your own inner thoughts, or agenda. Perhaps you are thinking about what to say next in the conversation, and therefore only half hearing what the other person is saying.

- In level two, you are intensely focused on what the other person is saying. They have your undivided attention and nothing is distracting you. Even your own ideas don't get in the way of hearing the other person.

- Level three is also completely directed towards the other person, but it has a wider focus wherein you are aware of more than just the words they are saying. You will perhaps notice their body language, the inflections and tone of their voice, their pauses and hesitations. You can feel them straining to avoid something or pulling towards something.

Your aim should be to listen at a minimum of level two and ideally at level three. Give people your full attention, ask open-ended questions and empathise with their perspectives and challenges. Pay attention to their feedback and use it to inform your actions and decisions. Listen to understand, not respond.

How you communicate, as well as when and to what level of detail, is an active decision in high-performing teams—they don't leave their communications to chance.

As well as ad hoc communication, high-performing teams have defined processes to ensure that everyone is on the same page. They might not realise it, but they are taking heed of William H. Whyte when he said: 'The great enemy of communication is the illusion of it'.[1]

High-performing teams excel at communication. In these teams, strong communication involves clear, transparent, two-way information sharing that engages employees, fosters collaboration and aligns with organisational culture and values. They avoid teams being communicated to, and operating in, silos thereby enhancing collaboration across the organisation. In doing so, they reduce the duplication of efforts and lack of coordination.

Fail to be intentional in your communication and employees become unsure about the company's goals, priorities or direction (or all three). A lack of intentional communication also creates confusion about roles and responsibilities, leading to tasks falling through the cracks.

In the absence of clear communication from leadership, people fill in the gaps themselves, often in a negative way. Rumours and gossip spread among employees and misinformation or speculation can create uncertainty, anxiety and distrust within the organisation.

Leaders of high-performing teams don't assume that everyone has understood a communication. They check that the behaviour of the team reflects what they have tried to communicate. If not, the communication did not work. They don't say 'I told them and they are still not doing it!' They find an alternative way to communicate the same message. In other words, they are under no illusion that every communication will be successful the first time and they know that simply saying something isn't the same as communicating it.

Ask yourself the following questions: Are your communications having the desired effect? If not, how are you going to do them differently and when are you going to make the change?

One Message Doesn't Fit All

Tell two people the same thing and they will interpret the information differently. They may read the non-verbal signals differently. They may understand the content differently. If they pass that information on, it will become more distorted.

Clearly, then, to avoid misunderstanding and to maximise the effectiveness of communication, it is important to tailor your communication for your audience.

I was once asked to speak in New York to a national sales force of approximately 300 people. When I was first booked, I was given a brief to deliver a motivational speech focusing on teamwork and the important role that a support team plays. The conference organisers were hoping to strengthen the relationships between the sales team and the back office staff. So I spent quite a while constructing a presentation to both inspire and strengthen the team.

When I arrived in New York three months later, I was told that there had been some 'restructuring' within the business. They were moving the customer service centre to another country and planning to reduce the number of employees. In fact, it was likely that half of the people who were about to listen to my motivational teamwork speech the following morning would be losing their jobs within six months! No wonder the meeting planner who had booked me looked a little nervous. There was no way I could deliver the speech I had planned. That night proved to be a long one as I rewrote what I was going to say.

The next day, as I entered the auditorium, I could sense the downbeat feeling amongst the delegates, but I delivered a speech that was tailored to their situation. Instead of talking about teamwork, I focused on coping with and embracing change. By the end of it, the crowd were on their feet, and there was a general buzz around the place for the rest of the day. The client was both relieved and delighted.

Effective communication is a fundamental driver of business success, contributing to enhanced collaboration, transparency and a positive work environment. Research supports that companies with high employee engagement, often fostered by strong communication, see a 23% increase in profitability and an 81% reduction in absenteeism, compared to those with low employee engagement.[2]

Communication as a Cultural Pillar

Salesforce, a cloud-based software leader, has developed a highly collaborative culture supported by open communication channels. Salesforce's internal platform, Chatter, functions much like a social media network for employees, enabling them to share updates, collaborate on projects and provide real-time feedback. This open communication tool plays a critical role in employee engagement: in fact, companies with effective communication practices are over 4.5 times more likely to retain top talent.[3] Chatter enables employees across departments and locations to stay updated, bridging any gaps in understanding.

Salesforce also hosts regular 'All Hands' meetings, a common practice among top companies, where executives communicate critical updates directly with employees and invite open Q&A sessions. According to a Gallup study, frequent and clear communication from leaders significantly improves employee engagement and productivity.[4] By prioritising these, Salesforce not only builds trust but also ensures all employees feel connected to the company's mission. The success of such communication practices is evident: Salesforce has repeatedly ranked among the top 10 best companies to work for, a testament to the power of open communication and employee alignment with the company's vision.

Emphasising Employee Voice

Southwest Airlines has cultivated a strong company culture, largely due to its emphasis on employee communication and feedback. Southwest's 'Communicate to Motivate' program is a key part of this approach, actively encouraging employees to share their ideas and feedback, which empowers them and reinforces their value to the company. Notably, research shows that organisations that prioritise employee feedback see an 8% increase in employee engagement and a 14.9% reduction in turnover.[5] This program ensures that employees feel empowered to voice their opinions, aligning the workforce with the company's goals and values.

Additionally, Southwest organises daily huddles. These are brief but effective meetings where employees discuss updates, set goals for the day and address any immediate issues. These daily huddles promote a culture of open communication, fostering collaboration and ensuring all employees are aligned on daily objectives. This type of structured communication contributes to Southwest's impressive employee retention rate, which is almost double the industry average. By embedding communication, Southwest has built a resilient, team-oriented culture that consistently receives high marks for employee engagement and satisfaction.

Modelling Communication and Transparency

Slack, a company synonymous with workplace communication, exemplifies the values it promotes in its products through its own internal practices. Slack's platform enables employees to communicate transparently through public channels, fostering a culture of openness and collaboration. The benefits of such transparent communication are well-documented: companies that maintain open communication channels are 3.5 times more likely to outperform their peers.[6] Slack encourages employees to discuss project updates, and provide feedback in real time, creating an agile and responsive work environment.

To further support open dialogue, Slack holds regular town hall meetings and Q&A sessions with executives, allowing employees to ask questions and discuss concerns directly with leadership. According to a survey by Harvard Business Review, 72% of employees report feeling more engaged when they can openly communicate with senior leadership.[7] By offering direct access to executives, Slack reinforces its commitment to transparency, fostering trust and ensuring that employees feel valued and informed.

Salesforce, Southwest Airlines, and Slack all demonstrate how prioritising communication can positively impact employee engagement, productivity and overall business performance. Companies that provide a clear onboarding process, driven by open communication, see better retention. In fact, research shows that 69% of employees are more likely to stay with a company for more than three years if they have a good onboarding experience.[8]

Take a moment before moving on to consider how open communication is at your organisation? Could there be more transparency between teams, as well as between senior leadership and other employees? How might you introduce that transparency, and how can you, on an individual level, start communicating more openly with your team?

In Conversation With Yvette Edwards, Director of Communications and Corporate Affairs at Unilever UK and Ireland, and Personal Care Europe

The bigger your organisation is, the greater complexity you're likely to face when it comes to communication both internally and externally. Few people know this better than Yvette Edwards, Director of Communication and Corporate Affairs at Unilever UK & Ireland, and Personal Care Europe. Unilever owns some of the world's best-known brands, ranging from Lynx, Marmite and Dove to Cif, Hellman's and Vaseline. I asked her what leaders need to know to deliver truly impactful and effective internal communications, especially if they're dealing with very different teams within a business.

MARC: *How important is internal communications in Unilever?*

YVETTE: It's very important, because we are a very big, complex organisation. The UK & I business is one of the biggest markets within Unilever. It's an exciting but complex footprint. In addition to the UK & I business, we have global research and development labs, and we have factories here in the UK. As a leader at Unilever, this means it's really important to think about all of your different audiences, what you are trying to land for each one, and how relevant it is.

Getting this right is crucial. In a very busy, fast-moving organisation, trying to get everybody on the same track and understanding what we're trying to do collectively is really key.

MARC: *You mentioned how complex the business is; I assume that you have an overarching framework for what the business as a whole needs to hear, but that is nuanced for specific areas?*

YVETTE: Yes exactly. In a big organisation, what's really important is that you start with your audience. I think sometimes people start with their specific message when actually everybody in the company needs to understand what it is that you are collectively aiming for.

At a macro level, there is a global strategy set out by the Unilever Leadership Executive and the Chief Executive, and everything that everybody else does in their part of the organisation needs to ladder up to that in some shape or form. In other words, you have multiple layers of communication.

At a macro level, this is the company strategy. This is what we're all aiming for. These are our targets. Then, at the country level or at the business unit level, you will break down what you need to do in your part of the organisation to contribute to the global organisational strategy.

In every piece of communication, there is a 'what' and a 'how'. The 'what' piece is all about strategy and growing the business. Then, the universal 'how' piece is around the values: what does it mean to work at Unilever and to be a Unilever employee? Its purpose is to coalesce people around a common set of values and behaviours which not only need to be shared from the top, but also need to be embedded locally. Because unless you know 'What does this mean for me?', it won't resonate properly.

MARC: *What do you want to see from a leader in terms of their communication?*

YVETTE: The most important thing for leaders is that they communicate, are visible, and lead well in their part of the business. They need to be visibly leading. Everyone wants clarity and simplicity from their leaders. We all need to understand, 'What does this mean for me?' That means the people you lead will be looking to you to interpret what your part of the business needs to do but in a really simple, clear way. The leader needs to know when to filter and where to amplify. In other words, you need to know what is important for your team versus what's not for your bit of the world.

Leaders also need to inspire and bring things to life. This is what other people in the business look to their leaders for. Communication is, therefore, a key leadership skill and a really important part of being able to properly help teams perform at their highest level.

MARC: *What does it look like when people aren't getting that right? And what do you do about it?*

YVETTE: It's a skill like anything else, and some of it you can learn. There are often two areas where people don't get it right. One is around tone. Sometimes people deliver a message, and they're thinking very much about the message and a bit less about the audience. You can have a really brilliant set of comms, but unless you've prepared and thought about how you're going to deliver the message, it doesn't always work. The second is content. It's really easy to overcomplicate things, to overshare, and then to leave your audience trying to work out, 'Which bit of that do I need to focus on?'

The way I help other leaders overcome this is to get them to start with the audience, not with the message. The easiest way to do that is by asking questions like 'Where is my audience at? What context are we in? Are people really happy, buzzing and ready to go?' If the answer to that last question is 'yes' then you know that you just need to fire up the engine and get people going. Or if the answer is 'no', it can help you recognise if you're in the middle of a difficult situation, or a change situation where you need to land your message in a slightly different way or at least acknowledge the starting point for the people you're speaking to.

That's sometimes when people get it wrong. They start with 'What is this thing that I want to share?' and not with 'Who is it I'm trying to share it with?' and 'How's this going to land?' Those are things that people can learn.

The other important element in this is tone. A big part of those in leadership getting communication right is about being authentic. I know 'being authentic' is a really overused concept and word at the moment, but it's so important to be yourself. People need to feel that you believe in the message or at least, if a message is difficult, acknowledge that it's difficult. It buys you a lot more credibility than just delivering something that feels like it's been written by someone else. Getting this right requires preparation. You have to think about what you say and how you say it.

MARC: *You said earlier that communication is a leadership skill, but we all have strengths and weaknesses in certain aspects of our work. Do you proactively support people who might need to build that strength?*

YVETTE: Definitely, you're right. Some people feel more confident communicating, and it's more in their comfort zone than it is for others, but like any skill, it's something you can learn. Whether we're talking about internal communications or external communications, the comms team in our business will always support the leadership teams or individual leaders with any internal engagements. That might mean practising or testing your messages with them or working out how to make things simpler.

Often the comms person is there to represent the employees and will say, 'How about we do it this way, or we make it a bit simpler?' It is a skill that you can learn if you practice and you have some expertise on hand to help you. When you have a comms team in a business, it pays to really lean on them to help you to get it right and improve your communication skills.

MARC: *Can we consider external communication for a moment? When I think about impactful external communications, I automatically think of the Dove Real Beauty campaign. How important is it to marry up that external messaging with the internal messaging?*

YVETTE: I think, almost without exception, Unilever employees are really proud of our brands. This is true whether we are talking about a brand that they're personally working on or not. Where there is a really big campaign, like the Dove Real Beauty campaign, that everybody can get behind, there is a marrying up of the internal and external. For example, each year, we have a Dove Day, where our employees can volunteer and run self-esteem workshops in local schools. I did it myself as part of a leadership team trip to France. One of my colleagues, who speaks excellent French, delivered the workshop in French with us non-French speakers helping from the sidelines. It was amazing to see how engaged the kids were with that messaging around appearance and perception, and how we perceive ourselves and others.

There is a big overlap in communication where you've got something that's a source of pride and in this case making the internal and the external feel consistent is really important. If you're saying or doing something externally that employees are not feeling internally, you're missing a massive opportunity. And vice versa. If you're saying something internally, and people are not seeing that reflected in how you talk to the rest of the world about your business, that's a gap too.

As you know, there is no real division now between internal and external communication. Employees consume all the same media as everybody else. So it's really important that the two at least don't contradict each other. You may say things slightly differently or share a bit more internally than you do externally, but they need to be aligned.

MARC: *I guess if you don't, there are all sorts of risks?*

YVETTE: Part of driving engagement is people having pride in the business and the good things that the business does. That applies whether we're talking about really strong performance, sustainability or brands doing something innovative and interesting. It's important to build that pride internally. One of the reasons people come to work is because they care about what they're doing and the more our communications can do to support this, the better.

MARC: *Is there any aspect of communication that you think your leaders need to be particularly mindful of?*

YVETTE: The starting point for any leader needs to be 'What's the outcome I'm trying to get to?', as opposed to, 'What's the message I'm trying to share?', because they are different things. It's important to ask yourself questions like, 'Am I informing, inspiring or involving? Am I trying to land a message which is not just information, but also trying to galvanise people behind a particular project or an idea? Or am I trying to involve people? Am I looking for feedback?'

That should really form the basis for what tone you need to communicate in. When you know the answers to those questions, it helps you work out what messages you need to land. The next questions to ask yourself are 'What am I asking them to think? What am I asking them to feel about this? What am I asking them to do with this information?' That's the bit to be mindful of. It's essential that you're really clear about why you're communicating this and what you want the response to be.

Of course, not every piece of communication requires this level of deep thought. It's fine if you're just sharing a bit of information like, 'Don't come into work tomorrow because there's too much snow. We're all going to work from home.' But it's important to recognise the difference between simple, informational communication and more strategic messages like, 'Here is our plan for the year. This is what we need to build. How are we going to collectively deliver this?' Those are two completely different bits of communication.

I'm being deliberately simplistic to make the point, but as a leader, you have to think carefully so that you're not over-communicating on something that just needs to be fairly straightforward, which risks confusing people. But at the same time, you have to make sure you're not under-communicating where you've got a much more complex job to do as a team, and you need people to come back to you, give feedback and help you to build or improve something.

MARC: *You mentioned feedback. Obviously, communication isn't a one-way process. How do you blend what you're receiving back from your employees into what you're doing?*

YVETTE: At Unilever, we have an in-depth employee survey. It gives us both quantitative and qualitative information. As a UK & I leadership team, we look at this and work out where we can address people's concerns. Can we address things that are frustrating people? Equally what is being done really well? What is motivating people? Can we amplify those?

So there's this formal feedback mechanism, but then there's also a cultural piece, which is around making sure that we have a healthy leadership culture. One of the other attributes in your model is psychological safety and that's also a vital part of the whole communication process. It's important to create the psychological safety for people to be able to share their ideas, to tell you what's working and what's not working from a communications point of view.

We hold UK & Ireland town hall meetings, which almost always include a Q and A session. The Qs and As are an important part of how we communicate. It means that the leadership team is not just talking about things they want to talk about, but that the floor is open to talk about things that are on other people's minds

MARC: *Is there anything else you would like to share with aspiring leaders?*

YVETTE: I think good communication, from a business point of view, is simple and repeated often. It's easy to assume, 'Well, I've communicated that now', but you have to make sure your messaging is consistent, and people are hearing the same message in different parts of the organisation.

Where it gets difficult for employees is if you have lots of different messages coming from different parts of the business and there is no proper air traffic control on internal communications. People can feel overwhelmed by the volume of what is being shared with them, and it becomes hard to pick out the most crucial and important things.

Different leaders, for all the right reasons, want to communicate their messages at the same time. But if you're on the receiving end, there's a risk that you end up not focusing on the most important or relevant things. So, for each piece of communication, you have to consider how relevant is this? Are you making sure that you're sharing it with the right audience? Or are you communicating to everybody something that's only relevant to a smaller proportion of people?

The final thing I would mention is the importance of understanding and acknowledging the context you are in at any given time. Our UK General Manager was amazing at recognising that a very different form of communicating was required during COVID, and he used much more personal style. He realised that sharing a little bit of himself went a long way. He would start every town hall with pictures of what he'd made in his kitchen that week, amazing dishes that he'd thrown together or a big curry that he'd made, which is not something you would do in normal times. But actually in those times, this was really important. It was a way of saying, 'We're all in the same boat, trying to manage this strange situation at home.' In that context, people really welcomed it. It then became easier to say, 'Okay guys, we still have a business to run, even though things are really tricky and difficult.'

When a leader is relatable, it often opens the door to people being willing to listen to everything else that they're saying.

There was a lot to take from that conversation. Here are my top three takeaways from my discussion with Yvette:

1. *Good communication is a skill you can learn. Creating clarity and simplicity in all your communications is the key to mastering this.*

2. *It's essential to align internal and external communications to ensure your employees aren't receiving mixed messages. As Yvette rightly points out, we're all consumers no matter who we work for.*

3. *Make space to listen to those in your teams. Understanding where your employees are will make it easier for you to tailor the tone of your messaging so you hit the mark more often than you miss.*

One of the challenges leaders can face is shifting their approach to different kinds of communication. Yvette gave some excellent examples of how easy it is to either over- or under-communicate depending on the circumstances. As a leader within a business, it is therefore worth considering communication in three ways.

Formal: Structured communications such as business updates, newsletters and company-wide announcements. These are typically owned by a communications professional and are clearly defined and coordinated.

Informal: Regular everyday conversations which happen organically during the day-to-day running of the business and can be encouraged by open door policies and tools like Slack or Teams. Whilst not controlled, it is important to ensure that everyone knows what is expected and what is not tolerated in terms of tone, language and general behaviour.

Designed: These are prearranged conversations that might be one-to-one, like in the case of an appraisal or as part of a team event. In both instances, some thinking in advance of the conversation will lead to better outcomes.

That approach helps with your individual communications, but what about communication within your team? After all, everyone, at every level, needs to be able to communicate openly and clearly if you are to create an environment for high performance.

Leaders as Coach

If this attribute is an area you've struggled with in the past, the following exercise can help unstick communication within your team and get everyone to be more deliberate in how they communicate with one another.

(continued)

(continued)

Process

A Team Communication Circle is a designed exercise you can use to improve communication within a team. This exercise promotes open dialogue, active listening and mutual understanding among team members.

1. **Set up the environment:**

   o Choose a quiet setting where the team can sit in a circle. When I run a session like this, I find it has the best impact when no desks or tables are in the way. This arrangement promotes equality and encourages open communication.

2. **Establish ground rules:**

   o We have removed the physical barrier of tables; next, we need to ensure the behaviours of those present encourage rather than inhibit. Set clear guidelines for the exercise, such as respecting each other's opinions, not interrupting when someone is speaking and maintaining confidentiality.

3. **Choose a facilitator:**

   o Someone must 'own' the process, so defining who will facilitate and guide the discussion is important. This needs to be someone who can 'hold their ground' when ensuring that everyone has a chance to speak and that the conversation remains constructive. If the team leader is overly dominant, this may need to be an external facilitator.

4. **Introduce the topic:**

   ○ Select a relevant topic or question for the team to discuss. My recommendation is to share this in advance so that those people who like time to reflect, and who are often the quieter ones in meetings, have time to do so ahead of the meeting. This could be related to a current project, a team challenge, or a general topic on team dynamics and collaboration.

5. **Round-robin sharing:**

   ○ Each team member takes turns sharing their thoughts on the topic. Encourage everyone to speak for a set amount of time to ensure equal participation. This will need clear facilitation, which is why the next step is so important.

6. **Active listening:**

   ○ While one person is speaking, the others are listening actively. This means giving full attention to the speaker, avoiding interruptions and not planning responses and justifications. This is listening to understand rather than listening to respond.

7. **Reflective responses:**

   ○ After each person speaks, the next person begins by reflecting on what they heard before sharing their own thoughts. This helps ensure that everyone feels heard and understood.

(continued)

(continued)

8. **Open discussion:**

   ○ After everyone has spoken, open the floor for a more free-form discussion. Team members should be encouraged to ask questions, seek clarification and build on each other's ideas.

9. **Summarise key points:**

   ○ At the end of the exercise, the facilitator summarises the key points and takeaways from the discussion. This helps reinforce the main ideas and ensures that everyone is on the same page.

10. **Follow-up actions:**
   ○ Ensure that any actions from the conversation are clearly defined and owned by the people present. Schedule a review session to address any unresolved issues and to continue moving the team forward.

Why It Works

This process is designed to achieve several things simultaneously.

Skills: It provides practice in active listening, clear articulation of ideas and respectful dialogue.

Understanding: Encourages team members to express their views and listen to others, leading to better mutual understanding.

Trust: Promotes an open and inclusive environment where team members feel valued and heard.

Collaboration: Facilitates better teamwork by addressing misunderstandings and aligning team goals and perspectives.

8

How Accountability Drives High-Performing Teams

I have already mentioned the need to empower people if you want to create and maintain a high-performing team. In conjunction with a culture of empowerment, high-performing teams have clear processes to enable people to take ownership of tasks and hold those people accountable for them. Teams that excel at accountability and ownership create a culture of trust, transparency and responsibility where employees contribute to the organisation's success.

Imagine a Formula 1 team on race day. Everyone in the pit knows their role: the commercial director who needs to keep the sponsors happy and the money flowing in, the driver who has memorised every corner and bump on the track and how to get the best out of the car and the engineers who have tuned that car to perfection and on race day need to make sure the tyres are changed and the car refuelled as quickly as possible. Each is trusted to deliver on their given task to the best of their ability, and each is held accountable for the delivery of that task. If one person does not hold themselves responsible, the whole team fails.

What does it look like when there is low accountability? When a team needs to improve its accountability and ownership, employees may blame others rather than take responsibility for their actions or outcomes. A lack of transparency in decision-making processes leads to crucial information being withheld or obscured, preventing team members from being held accountable. This is why open communication, as Yvette explained, is so important for driving high performance.

Understandably, a lack of transparency creates a toxic work environment without trust and collaboration. Without a sense of ownership over their work, employees produce subpar results or fail to take pride in their contributions. Consequently, projects consistently fall behind schedule or fail to achieve their desired outcomes.

Consider the role you have in your team. Are you taking ownership of all your responsibilities? Do you sometimes think, 'It's not my fault?'

Creating a Culture of Accountability

Which job in the world brings with it the most accountability? Doctor, politician, air traffic controller?

It is highly subjective, but for me, being a parent is the ultimate responsibility because you're shaping another person's life, character and future. Every action, decision and example you set impacts your child's growth and values. Parents' accountability to nurture, guide and protect is unmatched, as it influences their child's path well into adulthood.

Creating a culture of accountability is essential not just for your children if you have them, but for your organisation too, as you aim to maintain high standards and achieve long-term success. It ensures that employees take responsibility for their actions, meet performance standards and adhere to company values. Toyota and Amazon exemplify how fostering accountability can lead to operational efficiency, innovation and a commitment to company-wide goals. Each company implements accountability in unique ways, reflecting its specific culture, industry needs and corporate philosophy.

Accountability Through Continuous Improvement and Lean Manufacturing

Toyota's accountability model is deeply embedded in its 'Kaizen' philosophy, which centres on continuous improvement at every level of the organisation. Kaizen empowers employees to identify inefficiencies and propose solutions, reinforcing their sense of responsibility. This system is not limited to management; it is a fundamental part of Toyota's culture that emphasises accountability across all roles. Through Kaizen, employees can halt production if they detect quality issues—an approach that underscores individual responsibility for product integrity and operational efficiency.

Until 2014, Toyota used an Andon cord system, which allowed anyone on the production line to pull the cord and halt production. The word 'Andon' comes from the Japanese word for 'paper lantern' or 'burning lamp', referring to the flashing light that indicates the cord has been pulled.

Once production was halted, a team leader immediately asked why the rope was pulled. This prevented issues from propagating along the production line, making quality everyone's responsibility. The physical Andon Cord was phased out, but not the philosophy; it was simply replaced with a wireless version, an Andon Button. Accountability remains integrated into Toyota's workflow, where team members are not only allowed but encouraged to take direct action if they notice something amiss.

Toyota minimises errors and reinforces a collective commitment to excellence by empowering employees to take ownership of product quality. The Andon system has been instrumental in Toyota's reputation for reliability, showing that shared responsibility and accountability are crucial for achieving superior quality control.

Data-Driven Accountability and Ownership

Amazon places a strong emphasis on accountability through its 'Leadership Principles', which are central to its corporate culture. One principle, Ownership, encourages employees to think beyond their specific roles and consider the broader impact of their work on the entire organisation. Amazon expects its employees to make decisions with long-term consequences in mind, even if that means going beyond the immediate scope of their jobs. This fosters a sense of accountability and alignment with Amazon's strategic goals, as employees are motivated to act as stewards of the company's success rather than simply fulfilling isolated tasks.

Amazon also relies on metrics and data-driven decision-making to hold employees and teams accountable. Each department and project is measured by specific performance indicators, which are reviewed regularly to ensure alignment with Amazon's objectives. Performance reviews are conducted frequently, and managers use these metrics to evaluate individual and team effectiveness. This transparency in performance evaluation reinforces a culture of continuous improvement, as employees are encouraged to refine their approaches based on measurable outcomes. Amazon's metrics-based accountability model is a testament to its belief that quantitative assessments can drive consistent performance improvement and maintain high standards.

Common Themes and Lessons From These Accountability Models

While distinct, Toyota and Amazon's accountability models share a few common principles. Each company cultivates a culture of ownership, where employees are encouraged to take personal responsibility for their actions and contributions. Additionally, both companies emphasise transparency in their operations—whether through regular performance reviews, data-driven metrics, or direct employee involvement in quality control. This transparency helps create an environment where employees clearly understand expectations and can be held responsible for their actions.

Another shared trait is the use of feedback mechanisms to support accountability. Toyota's Andon Cord and Amazon's data-driven metrics provide employees with timely insights into their performance, allowing them to adjust their actions accordingly. Such systems ensure that accountability is proactive rather than punitive, enabling employees to recognise areas for improvement before issues escalate.

By making accountability an organisational value, these companies ensure that employees are aligned with corporate goals, motivated to maintain high standards and empowered to act in the company's best interests. This approach drives performance and cultivates a workplace culture where employees are deeply engaged and committed to their roles.

Take a moment to consider how you hold those on your team accountable. Do you have clear metrics that they work to? Are regular performance reviews built into your schedule? Is there a mechanism for employees to share concerns or ideas about quality improvements? If you're not sure where to begin, perhaps start with yourself. Can you set yourself a goal and ask your team to hold you accountable for it to get the ball rolling?

In Conversation With Dan Futter, CCO of Dow

Dow has twice been named as one of Fortune's World's Best Workplaces, most recently in 2024. I spoke to the organisation's Chief Commercial Officer Dan Futter about why accountability is so important for not only driving business performance, but also for creating a supportive and high-performing environment for Dow's employees.

MARC: *How important is accountability in your business?*
DAN: I'd say it's probably one of the things that we have to get most right. If you think about goals, you start

off with the mission for the company, you move down to the longer term goals and, if the process works well, those cascade down through the organisation. So, everybody eventually has their goals for that year and they line up with what the company is trying to do this year or over the next few years. Then, the accountability bit kicks in. How do you hit them?

You can get the alignment bit right and that's great, but it's worthless if you don't have the accountability for hitting the goal. So, for me, it's the second half of the discipline of goal setting that's most important. This requires an honest assessment of where those goals were realised and if you're not realising them, which you often aren't because you can't predict the world, then what are you learning from that? How are you adjusting? How are you going after the goals or thinking about the goals themselves? Were they realistic to begin with?

That's why, when you mentioned this book to me and the different attributes, I thought about accountability a lot, because it's the other side of the coin for goal setting. An organisation can't realise its purpose no matter what goals it sets unless it's got the accountability bit right.

MARC: *How does that manifest itself in the day to day of the business?*

DAN: Let's assume that the first bit is given, that the goal-setting cascade worked (which it doesn't always). From there, it's really about having a conversation. We have an annual goal-setting exercise, but I know what my goals were for the last five years, and I've got a fair idea what a chunk of them are going to be for the next five years because of the goal-setting cascade. So it's more of a realistic conversation with all of the people that you're going to have to work with to pull that off, and with your boss, who eventually will judge whether you did or not. This conversation is to make sure that the goals that you set are pragmatic and designed to achieve.

If I look at how I work with my people, I am talking to them all the time about the things they're working on because I try to create an environment where they come and talk to me about stuff that's bugging them. Or if they've got things they can't figure out, or challenges. Rather than giving me a ring every now and then for a victory lap, they're genuinely talking about where we are. Those daily conversations eventually roll into more formal, monthly reviews and then into quarterly cycles.

This means we can ask meaningful and valuable questions. Are we actually on track or not? Do we have to revisit this goal or revisit how we're going after getting it? It's a combination of structure and behaviour. The structure provokes you to talk about these things in a timely way, but also then the behaviour is about curiosity on the part of a leader, and the openness of the conversations that you can have. You need those good integrity conversations about whether we're getting there or not. We even have a phrase for it. It's called the 'say/do ratio'. You said X, and what did you do?

I do see it break down though, even though we talk about accountability a lot, because there might be 50 ways to look at one thing, and people can choose not to drill down to the one or two that are the leading indicators of how they're doing. In doing so, they can bury the inconvenient views and raise the convenient views about what was done. So, accountability can be super difficult to pin down. I'm conscious of that so I don't let that happen in my team. We focus on what really matters in terms of the metrics.

MARC: *You've articulated nicely how a team leader will support the team and get their team to think about being accountable. What does the individual have to do? And what is the organisation trying to create in terms of culture to encourage the individuals to hold themselves to account?*

DAN: The initial challenge is ensuring individual goals are lined up with something we're all trying to achieve. In a role like mine, where we're a support function for all of the businesses—in other words we're the pivot point between them, between commercial and finance on working capital, between commercial and manufacturing on supplier reliability, between commercial and supply chain—a big part of our job is the hard work at the beginning. That means making sure that when you set your goals, you're talking to all the other people who are going to be involved in delivering them. That's the hard yards piece of accountability. It's making sure you really understand what it is you're committed to, how you're going to measure progress and understanding all the people who might influence it.

My team works across those boundary lines where maybe they all agreed they were going to get something done at the start of the year but things have changed. The environment we're dealing with is super dynamic, so you have to make adjustments. That's when you need to have those realistic conversations that say, 'Alright this other team has had to reprioritise for good reason. How do we still keep things going, even though that's happening? How do we still make progress? Or do we just hold our hands up and say we can't do that now, until that problem goes away, and then we'll come back to it?'

We are trying to maintain a culture of honesty and not falling into the trap of excuse making. I see it happen, 'There are 100 reasons why I can't do this, and I can't control any of them so my goal is defunct'. No, you still find a way to make progress, to move the ball up the field, even with all these headwinds that we have to deal with. That brings us back to that ongoing dialogue, let's keep it real as we're progressing towards this target, but also let's reflect that from time to time, things change.

MARC: *You work in an industry that people outside like to have opinions on. If the external world is suggesting that your company could be more accountable, how does that impact the culture that you're trying to create within the business?*

DAN: Well, for sanity, forget about accountability! But in truth for sanity, the thing to do is rely on the data, the facts, because a lot of what we see externally is not fact-based or balanced. So, we focus on how we make things, the safety that we apply to it, what we think about emissions, how our products generally have a power for good and how we try to make them as circular or low footprint as they can be for water, nature or carbon, and keep falling back to the data.

When you think about accountability in those terms, you'd hope that when our people come through the door they see what we're saying has high integrity. The reason we sell this product, the reason people buy it, the reason they use it, is because it is, on balance, for the good. It improves society. It improves life. It improves health. When we look at corporate accountability, we of course obey the regulations in every jurisdiction that we operate in, but we tend to go much further than regulation. We set goals for ourselves on safety above and beyond whatever regulation demands, on emissions above and beyond, on whatever we do we go above and beyond.

We were the first company to set a net zero target in the chemical industry for carbon by 2050. We were the first to announce a major investment to decarbonise a full chemical facility up in Fort Saskatchewan, Ontario. We were the first to start bringing carbon to market and challenging the world to think about how decarbonisation gets financed and monetised. I work on that every day, and so that's real for me. There are another 30,000 employees that probably don't work on that every day, but I suspect that's just as real for them in terms of their sense of purpose and sense that what they do is for good.

MARC: *You must be pretty good at spotting a team where it looks like they lack accountability. What do you tend to see when that is happening?*

DAN: The first sign is excuses, and then it's wandering metrics. In other words, trying to find a new metric which makes you look good because the one we agreed on doesn't. The first is a behavioural indicator, the second means they're in a spin.

I would much rather the first behaviour be, 'Hey, we're struggling to hit this goal. Let's talk about why, and let's figure out how we're going to adjust'. But it's the obfuscation that happens that I've got no time for. The most obvious marker for me for spotting a lack of accountability is the convenient use of data and then finding an excuse when you eventually get pinned down for why you couldn't hit your goal. However, I don't think there's much benefit in publicly or directly exposing that. I tend to indirectly expose it by just focusing on the data and focusing on the behaviour I'd like to see mirrored.

I try to make sure that we stay concentrated so if we can't do it the way we thought, we figure out how we are going to get there in a different way. I tend to hit it indirectly because I can't get off the hook as my goals are linked to my team's goals. I make it a collective challenge, which it normally is rather than individual failing. I definitely don't call people out publicly or encourage the sort of humiliation that goes with it, but I do confront people in private.

I give a lot of public visibility, subtly, to the people who are hitting their goals. I highlight their work. I run a podcast internally, and I'll get them on a podcast so the whole company can hear about the good things they've done. We write articles all about them, the amazing results they've delivered, and how they went about it. So, I try to give lots of extraneous visibility to really good performance to drive that behaviour of accountability. As well as having a few private conversations and demonstrations by my own personal behaviour.

MARC: *When you're building a team, or you're bringing new people in, do you overtly look for those who demonstrate they can hold themselves accountable?*

DAN: I do. I focus heavily on questions about what they did to deliver a goal, especially in situations where I know they had to work with lots of other people. I want to make sure that I hear whether they choose to just focus on themselves or whether they choose to focus on themselves in context. I want to hear 'These people also did a great job. And I worked on influencing them', instead of just me, me, me.

I do want to know what they did, but I know they rarely did anything without somebody else. So, how did they influence the other person to make sure they were successful? Then, I focus on the projects where they didn't get it done, because I want to hear those same behaviours. 'How did you know you weren't getting it done? What did you do about it?' And I listen out for whether any excuses come out.

MARC: *Do you have some advice to give to somebody to ensure that their team's going to be able to hold itself to account?*

DAN: I think communication is king, and not making it an event. Make it something you're talking about all the time, and then consider how you recognise accountability. I can give somebody a salary raise, or I can give slightly more responsibility. People might see it, but it's more important to make sure that the person hears you praising them, in front of lots of other people, about how they delivered their results, or how a team delivered and how they contributed towards that great cultural shift you're looking for.

We meet together as a team, even if it looks like our goals are disparate, to see if there are any bridges between them and how we can help one another. I spend much more time influencing than I spend directing but trying to make sure that there is accountability for everything we're working on. And some I win, some I don't, but that's the goal.

Accountability starts at the top. People will mimic what they see from the most senior leaders, and if they see one crack of inconsistency in what people are doing versus what they're saying, that has a massive impact. This holds true whether it's at the high-level accountability of an organisation like ours on purpose-based activities, or down at my individual goals and watching how your own manager deals with their accountability. People will watch, and they're very clever at spotting inconsistencies and hypocrisies. So it can't just be an act. It has to be real.

Dan made some really interesting points about accountability at every level. Here are my top three takeaways from our conversation.

1. *Accountability is an essential second step after you've set goals if you want to have a realistic chance of achieving them.*

2. *It's vital to encourage open and honest conversations within your teams about their goals, whether they're*

on track and what they can do to overcome any challenges. Make these conversations part of your day to day.

3. *You can't expect the people you lead to hold themselves accountable if you—or others in leadership positions—don't. Start by making sure you are consistent and act with integrity, and you'll usually find others will follow.*

Accountability is more than owning up when you ate the last doughnut in the break room. It's about stepping up and not leaving the team hanging when things get tough. As Dan identified, it's about making accountability part of your daily conversations, rather than seeing it as an event that gets tied in with quarterly or annual performance reviews. As he also pointed out, leaders play a critical role in creating a culture of accountability, and therefore, the place to start is with yourself.

After all, if you aren't delivering, why should others? By setting clear expectations, modelling responsible behaviour, and offering support, you can help your team members become more accountable, elevating the entire organisation's effectiveness.

Leader as Coach

Developing a culture of accountability is vital if you are going to be a high-performing team. If it is lacking, then some form of diagnostic process will help determine where you are at and provide a direction towards improvement.

(continued)

(continued)

Process

An accountability ladder can help you understand where you and your team are on the climb to being fully accountable.

1. **Denial (bottom rung)**

    o *Behaviour:* Avoids responsibility and fails to recognise the issue. Typical statements include 'It's not my fault' or 'I didn't know'.

    o *Why accountability matters here:* It's hard to solve a problem when pretending it doesn't exist.

    o *Leader's role:* Gently point out the elephant in the room—prompt questions like, 'What could have been done differently?' to build awareness.

2. **Blame**

    o *Behaviour:* Recognises the issue but shifts responsibility to others or external factors. Statements include, 'They didn't do their part', often paired with, 'It's not my fault!'

    o *Why accountability matters here:* Blaming external factors prevents learning and improvement, hindering team cohesion and individual growth.

    o *Leader's role:* Leaders should encourage a shift in focus from what others did to what the individual can control. This can be done by helping them reflect on questions like, 'What actions could you take to improve this situation?'

3. **Excuses**

   ○ *Behaviour:* They know it's their job, but they've got a list of reasons why it went wrong. 'My laptop isn't fit for purpose. I tried, but it was too hard'.

   ○ *Why accountability matters here:* Excuses prevent progress and set a precedent for minimal effort, affecting personal and team performance.

   ○ *Leader's role:* Leaders can encourage individuals to consider how they might overcome obstacles rather than be hindered by them. Help them rethink with questions like, 'What would it take to get this done even with those challenges?'

4. **Wait-and-Hope**

   ○ *Behaviour:* Passively waits for change rather than actively pursuing it, with statements like, 'Maybe it'll be different next time. Let's kick the can down the road. Maybe next quarter?'

   ○ *Why accountability matters here:* Proactive behaviour is essential for driving results. Waiting delays progress and fosters a lack of ownership.

   ○ *Leader's role:* Leaders can empower individuals by encouraging small, manageable steps toward change. For example, 'What's one action you could take now to improve this?' promotes forward-thinking.

5. **Acknowledge responsibility**

   ○ *Behaviour:* Recognises personal accountability, saying, 'This is my responsibility, and I'll see what I can do'.

(continued)

(continued)

- ○ *Why accountability matters here:* This level is a turning point where individuals begin to embrace their role, setting the stage for real change.

- ○ *Leader's role:* Leaders can support this recognition by helping individuals create a clear plan for improvement and discussing potential actions they can take to address challenges.

6. **Taking ownership**

- ○ *Behaviour:* Takes full ownership of one's role and its impact on outcomes. 'I need to figure out what went wrong and improve it'.

- ○ *Why accountability matters here:* Taking ownership builds confidence and credibility, as individuals are now invested in outcomes.

- ○ *Leader's role:* Leaders can support ownership by providing constructive feedback and helping to set actionable goals. Statements like 'I appreciate your willingness to address this' can affirm the value of their ownership.

7. **Seek solutions**

- ○ *Behaviour:* Actively seeks ways to resolve issues, using language like, 'What can I do to improve this?'

- ○ *Why accountability matters here:* Solution-focused thinking drives creativity and improvement, vital for individual and team success.

- ○ *Leader's role:* Leaders can encourage a solution-oriented approach by offering resources and reinforcing the benefits of continuous improvement. For example, 'Let's look at some strategies together to prevent this in the future'.

8. **Proactive action (top rung)**

   ○ *Behaviour:* Embraces full accountability, taking initiative to prevent problems before they arise and leading by example.

   ○ *Why accountability matters here:* Proactive action builds a culture of responsibility and integrity within teams, inspiring others to act similarly.

   ○ *Leader's role:* Leaders can support individuals at this stage by recognising their initiative, providing leadership opportunities and encouraging them to mentor others. Statements like, 'Your proactive approach is a great model for the team', are helpful to encourage the continuation of this behaviour.

Why It Works

Using a structured framework like the accountability ladder helps individuals recognise their current level of ownership and take proactive steps toward responsibility. It encourages a shift from a passive or blame-oriented mindset to one of personal accountability and problem-solving.

9

How Goal Setting Maintains High-Performing Teams

Goal setting and accountability are intrinsically linked, as Dan correctly pointed out. There are numerous methods to determine and prioritise a team's most relevant goals, many of which come with acronyms like 'SMART' for Specific—Measurable—Achievable—Relevant—Time-bound or 'HARD' Heartfelt—Animated—Required—Difficult.

Regardless of how a high-performing team has determined its goals, they will be clearly defined and articulated so that all employees understand them. This is why the communication piece that both Yvette and Dan talked about is so crucial. Goals will also be aligned across different departments, teams and levels of the organisation. Priorities will be consistent, ensuring that everyone works towards common objectives that support the overall vision and strategy.

If a business is poor at goal setting and alignment, there may be confusion about the company's direction and priority tasks or projects. Employees may interpret the company's goals differently, leading to misalignment in efforts and wasted resources. This lack of clarity can result in unfocused efforts and difficulty measuring progress. Often a lack of clarity stems from a lack of open communication.

This is especially relevant to anyone involved in setting targets. Too often, leaders set targets based on a 'feeling' of what might be possible, like 'double-digit growth' or '5% growth in market share', and they forget to ensure that these targets serve the overall vision and strategy. Poorly set goals can result in unrealistic deadlines or targets that are difficult or impossible to achieve. Even if an employee or team hits their target, they can find themselves further away from reaching their vision.

If you reflect now, are you clear on your goals? Do you need help prioritising your work effectively? If the answer to either of these is yes, invest some time clarifying what you want to achieve.

Once you have a clear idea of what you want to achieve, you need to set out the steps and actions required to get there. In the world of business, and as I have already mentioned, acronyms like OKRs (objectives and key results) and KPIs (key performance indicators) are common enough to make their way onto a 'buzzword bingo' card—where people jokingly check off trendy business terms during meetings. However, OKRs and KPIs have gained widespread attention for good reason: they are powerful tools that many organisations use to set, track and achieve their goals.

The Origin and Purpose of OKRs

OKRs were developed in the 1970s by Andrew Grove, then CEO of Intel, to ensure that everyone in the company was aligned with Intel's larger strategic vision, especially during rapid growth. Grove's OKR methodology involves setting clear, ambitious objectives and identifying specific, measurable, vital results to gauge success. This framework helps create a results-oriented culture where everyone clearly understands what they are working towards and why. Grove's system also included periodic reviews to ensure that the company stayed on course and could address obstacles as they arose.

OKRs gained momentum outside of Intel in 1999 when John Doerr, a former Intel employee, introduced the concept to Google. Google adopted OKRs as a central element of its management approach, using them to align teams, set ambitious goals and maintain focus amid rapid expansion. Google's success with OKRs helped spread the concept across industries, where many organisations saw value in using them to enhance accountability, agility and productivity in their workplaces.

Meta's Use of OKRs for Alignment and Accountability

Meta (formerly Facebook) is one prominent organisation that has integrated the OKR framework into its operational culture. At Meta, OKRs align employees' daily tasks with the company's mission of connecting people. Each quarter, Meta sets new objectives that are ambitious but attainable, helping employees stretch toward meaningful goals while focusing on results that matter. Meta's use of OKRs has helped foster a culture of accountability; employees are encouraged to pursue challenging targets and continuously assess progress.

In addition, regular check-ins between team members and managers enable employees to adjust strategies as necessary, address any hurdles and stay aligned with the company's evolving priorities. This connects back to the need for clear and strong communication, as discussed with Yvette in Chapter 7.

An interesting example of Meta's approach to OKRs is how it extends its goal-setting advice to its users, particularly those using the Facebook Stars feature. This feature enables content creators to monetise their video and audio content. Meta advises creators to set achievable goals and track progress, mirroring the company's use of OKRs to set and achieve ambitious targets. In this way, Meta applies the OKR system internally and also promotes the framework to encourage success among its users.

Asana's Approach: Practising What It Preaches

Asana, a software company specialising in project management tools, takes a unique approach to OKRs by embedding them directly into its core product. Asana's platform is designed to help teams set, track and achieve goals, aligning with the company's use of OKRs. Within the company, Asana uses OKRs to define and pursue transparent objectives across the entire organisation. This transparency helps break down silos and creates accountability at all levels, as everyone can see the goals, track progress and understand how their contributions are moving the company forward.

For Asana, the OKR system is more than just a theoretical management tool—it's a daily practice. The company encourages structured planning sessions and regular progress reviews to ensure that employees are clear on their objectives and how their work contributes to larger company goals. Asana's regular updates and reviews allow teams to respond to new information, adapt to changing circumstances and continuously align their efforts with the company's evolving vision. This focus on adaptability and alignment illustrates how OKRs can support dynamic, goal-oriented work environments.

The Broader Impact of OKRs and KPIs

OKRs and KPIs each play distinct roles in business management but can effectively complement each other. While OKRs focus on setting ambitious goals and measurable results, KPIs are generally more specific metrics that track performance over time. KPIs allow organisations to assess ongoing operational effectiveness and pinpoint areas for improvement. Many companies use OKRs to set high-level goals and KPIs to monitor the metrics that reflect day-to-day success.

When companies like Meta and Asana employ OKRs, they invest in a culture of growth and accountability. When used alongside KPIs, OKRs give organisations the 'big picture' goals to aim for and the performance indicators to ensure that they're on track.

Do you have OKRs and KPIs in your organisation? If yes, now might be a useful time to check in on them. Look at each goal you have for yourself and your team. How was it set? What was the process behind deciding it? And the big question: does it get you closer to achieving your overarching organisational mission?

How OKRs Shape Business Success

Organisations using OKRs often see improvements in employee engagement and alignment with the company's mission. OKRs provide clarity, helping employees understand what they are working on and why it matters. Employees who see their work as part of a larger goal are often more motivated and engaged. For example, Meta employees know that their objectives support the mission of creating a connected world, which can provide a more profound sense of purpose. As Dan mentioned in our conversation, employees at Dow are also driven by a connection to a bigger purpose and sense of doing good in the world. It's also a key point that my next interviewee, Andreas Schierenbeck, CEO of Hitachi Energy, explores.

By implementing clear communication and alignment through OKRs, these companies demonstrate how effective goal setting can contribute to individual and organisational success. Whether it's Meta's ambitious quarterly goals, Asana's integration of OKRs into its core product, or Google's pioneering adoption of OKRs, the framework has proven to be a powerful tool for managing growth and driving innovation across industries.

In Conversation With Andreas Schierenbeck, Senior Vice President & Executive Officer, Head of Energy Business, CEO of Power Grids Business Unit, Hitachi, Ltd and CEO of Hitachi Energy

As the CEO of Hitachi Energy, which has committed $6 billion to expanding its capacity between 2024 and 2027, Andreas Schierenbeck knows about the importance of having targets. But his experiences at many organisations throughout his career have taught him that financial targets are not enough to drive true high performance. We discussed how goal setting needs to go beyond business goals and serve a higher purpose.

MARC: *How important is goal setting in your business?*

ANDREAS: In general, goal setting is important because budgeting and business planning rely on it. In any business you set targets to enable you to allocate costs, capital expenditure and many other things. But goal setting works in two ways. The first is in relation to planning—it provides a guideline for what you need to build up, perhaps what you need to avoid and how you have to move forward. The other side of goal setting is the motivational piece, where you want to set a challenging target, but not one that is too challenging.

You don't want to aim too low, because although that makes it easy to hit your target, you will miss out on a lot. But you also don't want to aim too high because that's demotivating—no one will run after a goal that is clearly not achievable. The key is to find the right balance between stretching individuals, teams and the organisation to encourage performance, without overstretching by setting unattainable goals.

MARC: *How do you find that balance? What kinds of conversations are you having with your senior leadership teams to get that balance right?*

ANDREAS: If you talk purely about budgets and figures, you're looking at a negotiation process with your supervisory board. But goal setting is not only about figures and hard facts like revenue, profit and margins. There are parts of the organisation, like developing new business, moving into a new market or pushing into a new area, where you need what I would call softer targets.

This is where you can be a bit more flexible and take the conversation into team building and creating a strong vision where you say why you are doing what you're doing as well as what you want to do. This is when you can think outside the box and say, 'Wouldn't it be great if. . .' and 'What is necessary to achieve that?'

MARC: *You've obviously got your organisational targets, which your team and people work towards, but the world that you work in is also linked to reducing carbon emissions. Those* *targets are set externally to you, and you have no control over them, so how do you address that?*

ANDREAS: You're right, but for me that is an example of another target beyond the financial that you have to factor in. I'll share an example from one of my previous jobs to demonstrate why just working to financial targets isn't enough. When I joined thyssenkrupp Elevator in 2011 (now TK Elevator), I was told to achieve $1 billion in profit, and 15% profitability for the business. They were purely financial targets. But after about two years of running to purely financial targets, I realised it would never work. A service mechanic who is charged with maintaining 100 elevators every year isn't going to get up in the morning because they want to contribute to $1 billion profit or maintain profitability at 15% because that's completely meaningless for them.

The other challenge was that, at this time, the organisation was actually five businesses: elevators, escalators, passenger boarding bridges, home elevators and stair lifts. These have nothing in common. They have different regulations, different behaviour, different teams, different everything. The trick was to create a common vision and common culture. To do that, we had a lot of discussions about what ties us together. From those, we came up with 'urban mobility'. We're transporting people from the plane to the airport, the airport to the Metro, the Metro to your home in a high-rise building, and for those with limited mobility from one part of your home to another.

Having a common vision—we do urban mobility—allowed us to drive innovation. For example, being the first company to have elevators driven by linear motors rather than ropes, or having the first solutions for service technicians based on Microsoft machine learning. These are all fascinating developments, and they're things you can connect to emotionally. As we rolled the vision out, we broke it down into targets we could achieve. That worked really well, because all of a sudden we weren't running after financial targets. Instead, we were running for a joint culture and softer targets, which made everyone more prepared to go the extra mile.

MARC: *I know you often talk about the need for that higher purpose in an organisation. I saw recently that you've set new targets within Hitachi Energy that will have an impact both for the business and decarbonising the energy sector. How does that come together?*

ANDREAS: As soon as you talk about that path, I think you're already there. So we're not only doing business because we're selling transformers, high-voltage switch gear and high-voltage direct current (HVDC) and so on; I believe we are helping the world to electrify and decarbonise, so we're contributing to that external target. I see us as having an enabling function—it's not so much about driving the technology as it is about driving society into decarbonisation as an enabler. It's one thing to say we've completed an HVDC link, but it's another to say we have enabled X number of households to have green electricity coming from wind farms. That's what I mean when I talk about having a higher purpose.

We are expanding to follow our markets and our customers and to help them go the extra mile. But we're not doing that because of financial targets. In fact, we could probably have achieved our financial targets more easily without expanding so much. But that higher purpose encourages all of us to do more.

MARC: *I'd like to switch slightly and ask you about your personal targets. In amongst this huge machine that you're part of, what do you set as personal targets?*

ANDREAS: That's always a tricky question and it can be hard to find, but I'm always looking to make a difference and encourage cultural change, so that's my target. Sometimes that's hard to formulate, but I frame it by asking myself, 'What is the organisation and business I find? And what is the organisation and business I want to leave behind?' For me that's how I can make a difference and leave a legacy. Steve Jobs said he wanted to 'make a dent in the universe' and I don't know that I'd go down that route, but it's a similar concept.

For every assignment I've done, I have left something behind. I'm talking about something that reminds me and others of what we as a team have achieved. And although it's early days for me at Hitachi Energy, this is what I want to achieve. I want to make a change, to see a transformation and to leave something behind to create a better organisation than the one I stepped into. I want to create alignment with the environment, the people and the culture to help achieve these targets for the greater good.

My main purpose is always to make a difference. It's not about managing figures—in the kinds of businesses I work in, the figures are so huge that you can't connect to them. They just become figures on a spreadsheet that don't mean anything to you. Just like my elevator service mechanics, I need a goal I care about.

MARC: *I like the way you articulate what your goals are and how you think about making an impact. How do you translate that to the people who are delivering on the ground?*

ANDREAS: This is a rather complicated process. When you start a new assignment, you have to learn about the business at the organisation. That goes hand in hand with the market, your customers, your colleagues, what you see and where the market should go. It can be rather complicated to find out what you need to know.

Sometimes you have to go to your customers and ask them, 'What do you expect from us?' So, when I was at thyssenkrupp Elevator (now TK Elevator), I asked the architects and consultants, 'What do you expect from us as an industry?' By asking that question, I found it was something completely different than what we had assumed as engineers. So getting these connections between markets, customers, society, financial targets, what you assume and what the organisation assumes, makes the process fascinating. From there, you can derive targets and then you have to convince your colleagues that these are the right targets.

We all have the tendency to only look at our small part, and not look further. Sometimes we have to broaden our perspective a bit. Some people will feel this in their gut and will be relatively easy to convince; others may need more information. But for me, the interesting part of setting goals is getting into that process of thinking about the customer, society and colleagues.

MARC: *When I think of goal setting, the other side of the coin is accountability and holding people to account to those goals. How do you make sure those things are side by side?*

ANDREAS: I think when you've achieved the right vision and everyone agrees on where you want to go, you can put intelligent targets behind that vision. There are two ways to do that: either you set the targets or you ask for targets. For example, we've just founded a new business unit for service, and we have an organisational target of wanting to grow the business three times compared to where we started. But I've told the Managing Director of the new business unit to talk to their team and come up with their own targets.

I told them that I could give them a target, but that it's probably better for them to go away and think about what will stretch the envelope. When you empower teams like this, you get better buy-in. It's a really good exercise to get people to think outside the box about what could be achievable, and what is good enough that I will accept it.

MARC: *I like that, and as I'm listening to you I feel that the challenge is that if you just ask them for a target, sometimes they don't make it big enough, but if you ask them what success looks like then they might stretch a bit further, and it sounds like you're having those conversations.*

ANDREAS: Exactly, this approach gets more buy-in. If you ask them to start thinking about what success looks like, and asking questions like, 'What is the right number? What is barely achievable but still achievable? And how can we do that?' then they start thinking about the process before you set any targets. That's important because if you just give them a target, they might look at it and then forget it. Or they might not approach it in the most efficient way.

I think of this a bit like flying a plane—if you're driving too fast and too high, you're not getting any more drive to lift the plane up after a certain point; in fact, you're losing everything.

MARC: *Is there anything else you'd like to add in relation to goal setting?*

ANDREAS: From my perspective, it's important that you separate hard, financial targets from the other part of what doing business is about. You don't drive a business to the next level with only hardcore financial targets. You need more than that. You need a vision. You need buy-in much more than just the right numbers. You have to get emotional buy-in from your colleagues, and that definitely means you need something more than figures and money.

You have to create this magic area where everyone you work with can look at what you're doing in the organisation and think, 'It would be great to do that. It's something to be proud of and something which can last'. I want people to be working on things that they're proud to tell their family and friends about, even if their friends and family don't fully understand the intricacies of the work.

My conversation with Andreas provided some fantastic insights about goal setting, and particularly about the need to make it emotional as well as data-based. Here are my top three takeaways from our conversation:

1. *Goal setting isn't just about facts and figures. It's an essential tool for motivating everyone in an organisation to perform at their best.*

2. *Targets don't just have to be set internally. Organisations can anchor to external targets, like supporting decarbonisation, and make them a part of how they operate and do business.*

3. *Asking people to set their own targets to align with a compelling vision will create far more buy-in and often lead to much greater success than if targets are handed down from senior management.*

Unsurprisingly, and as you've heard from both Andreas and Dan, leaders play an essential role in goal setting regarding the team's overarching goals and creating an environment where individuals proactively set their targets in line with the team's purpose.

It's worth considering standardising your goal setting by using a methodology like OKRs or SMART goals. This reduces the likelihood of falling into the 'finger in the wind' arbitrary goal-setting approach I mentioned earlier.

Whatever framework you choose, you must ensure that objectives are clear and that individuals are aligned with the team and organisational objectives. Connect all your goals to your bigger vision, as Andreas explained, and you'll find people put in much more effort than if they are focused purely on business figures. Goals need to be visible to all stakeholders to foster accountability and collaboration. Progress has to be tracked through frequent reviews, and honest conversations, while ongoing feedback drives continuous improvement.

Leader as Coach

Harvard Business School professor Dr John Kotter introduced his change model in his 1996 book *Leading Change*.[1] Since then, numerous leaders have adapted it to suit their needs, often referring to it as a process of vision to action. Below is a vision-to-action exercise to improve goal setting within your team.

Process

Vision to action workshop

1. Define the team vision:

   - Discuss and define the team's long-term vision. The vision should inspire and provide a clear direction for the team's future. At this point, an excellent question is, 'What does success look like?'

2. Break down the vision:

   - Once everyone is clear on the vision, the next step is to break it down into the major milestones towards achieving this vision. The important thing at this stage is to avoid getting caught up in the minor details.

3. Solution session:

   - Consider each milestone and discuss specific actions, projects or initiatives that could help achieve it. Aim to keep everyone open-minded about how to work towards this milestone. A 'that will never work' attitude will limit the group's creativity and lead to suboptimal solutions.

4. Prioritise ideas:

   - Prioritise the generated ideas based on impact and feasibility, selecting those that will make significant progress toward the milestone.

5. Develop action steps:

   - For each prioritised idea, develop detailed action steps outlining what needs to be done, who will be responsible, and any required resources.

6. Create a roadmap:

   - Create a comprehensive roadmap that includes all the prioritised ideas and action steps. Organise the roadmap logically, aligning it with the team's overall

(continued)

(continued)

vision. A visual representation can help with discussions and tracking progress.

7. Assign responsibilities:

   - Assign team members or sub-teams to each action step. Again, clearly define roles and responsibilities to ensure accountability.

8. Set timelines:

   - Establish timelines for each action step, including start dates, deadlines and critical inflection points. Ensure that these timelines are realistic and allow for flexibility.

9. Regular check-ins:

   - Schedule regular check-ins to review progress, address any challenges and make adjustments as needed. These check-ins help keep everyone aligned and accountable.

10. Reflect and adjust:

    - Conduct a regular reflection session to evaluate progress, what works well and what could be improved. Use these insights to adjust and refine future goal-setting exercises.

Why It Works

Conducting a vision-to-action session, as outlined here, fosters creativity, alignment and a strong connection between the team's daily activities and their long-term vision.

10

Why Recognition Maintains High-Performing Teams

Recognition naturally follows on from accountability and goal setting. After all, this is a form of feedback and you can't hope to achieve your goals or hold people accountable if you don't recognise their efforts. Overall, businesses that excel at recognition and appreciation create a positive work environment where employees feel valued, respected and motivated to perform at their best, all of which supports their efforts to achieve ambitious goals. Recognition efforts contribute to higher levels of employee engagement, satisfaction and productivity, ultimately driving organisational success.

The obvious way to recognise people is that attractive carrot—money. But money isn't necessarily the best motivator. You need much more than financial recognition to sustain a team's motivation—both Andreas and Dan alluded to this in our conversations. Of course, most people need an income; otherwise, they would stop working, but that financial gain can become a negative issue all too quickly.

How often do you hear people talk about their salary in a positive way? It is far more likely that you have heard them say 'I deserve more' or 'they don't pay me enough' or 'did you hear what bonus the sales team got, it just doesn't seem right'?

Salary is the 'sugar rush' of recognition. To sustain motivation and performance, a more nuanced process is required, a steady and consistent release of energy.

Take time to understand how a team wants to be recognised. Is it a celebration of success when a goal is achieved? Or is it as simple as saying thank you when people have gone the extra mile to support others? This is a topic I talk about with Caomihe Keogan, Chief People Officer at AVEVA, a bit later in this chapter.

When a business is poor at recognition and appreciation, employees feel undervalued leading to decreased job satisfaction and overall morale. They become disengaged and less motivated to perform at their best, and if there is obvious disparity across the team, it leads to resentment and conflict.

With appropriate and considered recognition, people go above and beyond in their roles and take initiative to improve processes or solve problems.

How do you recognise the efforts of others in your team? Do you facilitate peer-to-peer recognition? How about recognition for teams and individuals at an organisational level? Can you think of other ways to show your appreciation for the work they do?

What Does Strong Employee Recognition Look Like?

Google and Southwest Airlines each demonstrate the power of strong employee recognition programs in fostering a supportive, motivated workplace. Google's recognition initiatives, such as 'gThanks', allow employees to publicly celebrate each other's efforts, cultivating a collaborative atmosphere. The platform enables peer-to-peer acknowledgments, making it easy for employees to highlight colleagues' contributions in real time. Formal programs like 'Googlegeist' recognise exceptional achievements across the organisation, providing employees with an incentive to excel. These programs contribute to high employee satisfaction, promote motivation and underscore Google's commitment to valuing individual impact.

Southwest Airlines, known for its vibrant company culture, has a similarly effective approach to recognition. Programs like the 'Winning Spirit Awards' reward outstanding performance, reinforcing the company's values and goals. Southwest's 'SWAG' (Southwest Airlines Gratitude) platform is designed for employees to recognise one another's efforts, creating a sense of community and appreciation. In addition to these formal programs, Southwest also emphasises personal touches—leaders frequently send handwritten notes or share personalised acknowledgements, deepening connections across all levels of the organisation.

Programs like 'gThanks' and 'SWAG' may have catchy names, but effective recognition programs don't need to be cleverly branded. What's essential is that companies establish channels for authentic appreciation, as these initiatives drive higher engagement, job satisfaction and productivity. Recognition programs help employees feel valued and motivated, contributing to a more positive and resilient workplace culture.

The Value of Peer-to-Peer Recognition

Intuit is a leading financial software company, recognised globally for products such as TurboTax, QuickBooks and Mint, which help individuals and businesses manage their finances and taxes. Founded by Scott Cook and Tom Proulx in 1983, Intuit has a culture that places a high value on innovation, collaboration and, importantly, employee recognition. Cook's vision emphasised creating a supportive and inventive environment where employees felt their contributions were valued, a philosophy that persists in the company today.

To honour this commitment, Intuit established the 'Spotlight Recognition Program', a platform where employees can nominate colleagues who exemplify company values or make meaningful contributions. This peer-to-peer nomination system reinforces the sense of community and camaraderie within the organisation, as employees are actively encouraged to recognise and celebrate each other's achievements. Recognition is then shared widely across the company, amplifying each achievement's impact and providing motivation to others.

Beyond peer recognition, Intuit also has a formal awards program, the 'Scott Cook Innovation Awards', named after its co-founder. This award specifically highlights employees who have made significant contributions to innovation at the company, honouring Cook's legacy and the company's dedication to continual improvement. Recipients of this prestigious award are recognised company-wide, which not only bolsters employee morale but also encourages a forward-thinking mindset. In addition, Intuit frequently recognises employees publicly during company meetings and on its internal platforms, ensuring that recognition is an integral part of the corporate culture rather than a sporadic gesture.

Online retailer Zappos is famous for its distinctive workplace culture, rooted in values of fun, family spirit and employee happiness. Founded by Nick Swinmurn and later led by Tony Hsieh, Zappos emphasises customer service and employee satisfaction, believing that happy employees lead to happy customers.

It too has created a program to encourage peer-to-peer recognition. Hsieh advocated for a corporate culture that empowered employees to bring their authentic selves to work, creating an environment that prioritised mutual respect and support.

Zappos' commitment to recognition is evident in programs like the 'Coworker Bonus' system, where employees can give $50 bonuses to peers as a way to acknowledge exceptional teamwork, helpfulness, or dedication. This system allows for spontaneous, informal recognition, enabling employees to celebrate achievements and recognise positive behaviours immediately. By providing this option, Zappos fosters a sense of ownership among employees, empowering them to reinforce the behaviours and values that contribute to the company's success.

The company also offers 'Hero Awards', which are given to employees who demonstrate outstanding service or go above and beyond their regular duties. These awards highlight Zappos' commitment to recognising not only individual contributions but also to cultivating a supportive, service-oriented culture. Hero Awards recipients are celebrated publicly during company meetings, ensuring that their efforts are acknowledged company-wide, reinforcing a sense of pride and community.

In addition to structured recognition programs, Zappos regularly celebrates achievements through events and fun gatherings. For example, they may organise themed parties, surprise celebrations or other events to honour individual or team milestones. These celebrations are deeply embedded in the company's DNA, creating a work environment that is not only productive but also enjoyable and engaging.

Prioritising employee recognition builds workplaces where employees feel valued, respected and motivated. Companies like Intuit and Zappos demonstrate that when employees feel appreciated and acknowledged for their efforts, they are more likely to contribute positively to the company's success.

Pause here and think about how you can include more recognition within your team. Could you start your weekly team meeting with a call for shout-outs for good work from the previous week? Or perhaps you could set up a shared doc so that employees can recognise one another in real time? You'll likely find some inspiration for increasing recognition in my next conversation too.

In Conversation With Caoimhe Keogan, Chief People Officer of AVEVA

World-leading industrial software provider AVEVA has developed interesting and highly successful ways of recognising its employees beyond simple financial rewards. I spoke to Caoimhe Keogan, Chief People Officer at the company, to learn more about what she's seen work well and how other companies and teams can introduce greater recognition into their day to day.

MARC: *Recognition can be a cultural pillar as well as a leadership behaviour. Do you think you need a formal system for recognition?*

CAOIMHE: I don't think you necessarily need a formal system when you're building a company from scratch. You can be very intentional about how you shape that culture. Do I think there are likely organisations out there where recognition is a really strong part of their culture, and there's not necessarily formality around the processes? Absolutely. I'm sure that probably is the case because you could build it into the core DNA of a company as a founder. But if you take a different construct, like the organisation that I'm in, where the company has been put together over multiple years with lots of acquisitions and is of significant scale and size, you do need some form of structure. Based on feedback from our employees, we've been focused on trying to improve recognition within the culture of the company and have done so through defining processes and having a framework of ways in which we recognise our people.

MARC: *Can you explain a little bit more about the framework? Is it focused on individual recognition? Is it around team recognition? Is it around geography? How do you do it?*

CAOIMHE: There are a couple of different ways. The basic, most informal way is via our peer-to-peer recognition platform. It's enabled by a technology platform that allows people to give peer kudos. It's non-financial and is about pure appreciation for a colleague. You go to the platform, and you congratulate a person or a team for an achievement, write some kind words and maybe attach a GIF. It's a virtual high-five or kudos. Everybody reports that they like getting that email in their inbox that says, 'Hey, you've received some recognition'. I mean, who doesn't get a little hit of dopamine when you click through to see that somebody's taken the time to write something nice about something you've done? It's a platform that you can go to at any time and all the recognition is public. From time to time, I grab a coffee and cheer myself up by browsing through all of the colleagues' comments.

Then, there is individual recognition and feedback on performance. This is the relationship that people have with their managers, one on one. Over the last few years, we've moved away from a traditional performance year-end review. We now have three formal check-ins a year, including one at the end of the year, where managers sit down with their individual team members. It's very much geared towards a conversation about how they're doing, not just from a performance perspective but also from a well-being and developmental perspective.

We don't have a performance rating. We have taken those high-anxiety elements out of those conversations and the check-in doesn't result in a score. The idea is that we have frequent check-ins, where you discuss performance, goals for the next period of time, and how you're doing holistically, including personal well-being, as well as talking about career aspirations. It's a broad range of conversations, and these frequent check-ins provide an opportunity for managers to give recognition at an individual level.

MARC: *Is there a financial element to recognition at this point?*

CAOIMHE: Once a year, there is the formal financial element of recognition. The way in which our compensation philosophy works is that everybody has a base pay, which compensates them for their skills and experience in the market, and the market value of their job. Then, we have an individual bonus scheme on top, where managers have the ability to exercise some discretion around the level of bonus that they give to people as a reflection of the prior year's performance and impact.

MARC: *Is there then a functional level to your recognition framework?*

CAOIMHE: Yes, taking it to a functional or departmental level, sales, marketing, product development, R&D, finance, HR etc., all have their own team awards and recognition. Most of them run quarterly and are again usually peer-based nominations for awards and recognition, and then involve a selection process by the leadership of that function.

So, with my own team, for example, once a quarter we have a People Team all hands call. Everybody who works in the team comes to that call. Although saying that, we actually do two calls with the same content repeated, because we're so globally distributed that you can't get people across all the time zones onto one call! It's not good for people's well-being.

On these calls, we typically recognise three individuals and a team for going above and beyond or doing something exceptional. There's a big celebration on the call, lots of kudos and congratulations. There's a little bit of a token financial award with it as well. And people like it. They get a certificate. Sometimes I see them posting it on LinkedIn because that level of recognition means a lot to people.

Finally, we have our live global annual recognition event, which we call our Global People Awards. Again, anybody can nominate anybody in the company for an award. I think this year we had over 800 nominations out of 6,000 employees. There are eight different categories of awards, and we use an external company to support us through the process. They help us sift through the nominations in each of the categories and evaluate submissions with some independent scrutiny.

Then, we create a shortlist and make a big deal of it, publishing it on the company intranet. The winners are kept under wraps until the event, when we run the live global broadcast, hosted by myself and the CEO. It's a full production, a bit like The Oscars (on a very tight budget)! Winners usually get a prize that includes some meaningful financial recognition, but again feedback is that it's the acknowledgement that means more than the money. This event is very high profile internally and our teams gather together in various offices around the world to watch it live.

I should also note that not all recognition processes where we want to reward people involve just giving an additional cash bonus. One of our other annual processes is our CEO Awards, which are manager-nominations for individual high performance, which is then endorsed at Executive level. This recognition results in an element of investment in the person's development. So, you get a certain amount of money to go and spend as you choose, but you also get a similar amount which is ring fenced to take a training course, get some coaching, or invest in your career development in another way.

MARC: *I'm interested in how you perceive the impact. You have talked about both financial and non-monetary recognition. Where do you see the best impact?*

CAOIMHE: It's hard to know, but research would support the fact that financial recognition can be nice but is not necessarily as effective. I think it depends on an individual's circumstances. Clearly, if someone is in a lower income bracket, you might be able to give them some financial recognition that is really quite meaningful for them and their family. For the most part though, as a high-knowledge worker employer, I would say the financial awards that we do are more of a gesture to reinforce or underpin the fact that we are saying thank you in a more formal and meaningful way.

When you consider financial recognition in terms of an annual bonus scheme, if that's an established practice within a company, people come to expect it over time. That's just human nature. If it's tied to overall company financial performance, as is the typical prudent financial governance of a company, it can be hard for some people to connect their personal efforts to that financial outcome. So what tends to happen is that when the company hasn't had a good year, performance wise, you end up having to manage unhappy people who may have personally worked very hard. In other words, sometimes it can be a demotivator.

I'll give you a personal example of how to make financial recognition more impactful. Earlier in my career, something happened where I went above and beyond for a sustained period of a month or two. My boss came down to my desk with balloons and an envelope. Inside was a voucher for a trip away for me and my kids! He could have given me the equivalent monetary value as a bonus, but if he had I wouldn't be telling the story 10+ years later.

What I remember is that he recognised what I had done. The extra work had taken me away from my young family. He wanted to give me the time back with my kids who were really young at the time. He wanted me to go and have an experience with them. He said, 'You decide what it is, but we are going to organise it for you. Tell my assistant where you want to go and she's going to book it for you, and you are going to go away with your kids'.

That for me is an example of how you really recognise people. It's 'I see you'. It's personal. It's connected. It takes a bit more effort and trying to figure out how to do that at scale is hard, but it can be done. At another of my previous companies, we had annual employee awards where, because we were smaller, we were able to get everybody together at year-end in one place. We knew in advance who the employee winners were and came up with very personalised awards for all of them. We had so much fun with it. There was a team of people who had to go and investigate what would be meaningful to that person, without giving the game away that that person had won.

I remember a colleague becoming emotional on stage when we told her what she had won. We had found out that over the previous 12 months she had been trying to renovate her garden. It was very important to her. So, her prize was for a landscape gardener to come in and finish transforming her garden. Being able to personalise recognition like that is way more powerful than if we'd said you're getting a cheque for £X,000. Money is great, but it goes in, and it goes out again.

MARC: *So, personalising can be really impactful but not everyone is comfortable with recognition, are they?*

CAOIMHE: The research would suggest that people feel differently about whether they get recognition in private or in public. And I have definitely come up against people who feel quite uncomfortable with being called out publicly and thanked. They would rather it was a private one-to-one recognition.

However, many people do enjoy sharing their own and others' successes. The social media posts that we did on LinkedIn after our last Global People Awards were the best-performing social media posts we did all year. We do a lot on LinkedIn as a business, and it's not always about the people agenda. We also do business development, content around our product, around our customers, and around partnerships. But the best-performing social media were the posts where we were sharing photos and shout outs from our People Awards. It helps with our brand as an employer, but it also helps with business development because our customers will see a positive aspect of our culture.

MARC: *Just to finish then what advice could you give to anybody who wants to improve recognition within their organisation? Maybe something for someone who's just taken on a role as a team leader or an HR professional.*

CAOIMHE: At a simple level, the power of a thank you is huge, and you have to do a lot of it before it's too much. In fact, I'm not really ever sure you can say thank you too much. I probably don't thank my team enough. We all have that feeling of, if we keep thanking people, recognising them, and saying they're doing great, maybe it becomes meaningless. Perhaps you can overdo it to the point at which it becomes meaningless and trite. But I think most of us are a very long way away from overdoing it to that extent. I'm pretty sure most of us could do a lot more of it if we took the time.

The other thing that's really interesting is to ask people how they like to be recognised. We often assume that the way in which we like to be recognised is how others like to be recognised too. If you're a team leader, understanding that about your team is very helpful, and when you can tailor your recognition to each individual, you will have more impact.

Here are my top three takeaways from my conversation with Caoimhe:

1. *Peer-to-peer recognition is very powerful, and finding a way to facilitate that within your organisation can go a long way towards creating engaged, motivated and high-performing teams.*

2. *Personalised gestures often mean far more than financial recognition. By taking the time to get to know the people on your team, you're not only thanking them for their work, but also showing you care about them as individuals.*

3. *Don't underestimate the power of saying 'Thank you'. It's free, and as Caoimhe says, it's very hard to say it too much.*

As we've heard from Caoimhe, and seen from the other examples I shared earlier in this chapter, focusing on recognition within your team can significantly enhance employee morale, productivity and overall job satisfaction. One of the key takeaways here is that recognition doesn't have to be financial and in fact is often most effective when it isn't! Be it a formal public acknowledgement, something personalised and discreet, or a simple thank you, good leaders ensure that people feel recognised and appreciated. They also encourage everyone to recognise good work when they see it. This, for me, is one of the keys to unlocking high performance through recognition— ensuring that it's part of your team's culture for everyone to say thank you and highlight when people go above and beyond, rather than waiting for that recognition to come from management.

Leader as Coach

A simple yet effective exercise to improve recognition within a team is to create a 'Spotlight Session'. This provides a structured opportunity for team members to express appreciation for each other's contributions.

Process

Introduction to the session:

The leader should begin by explaining the purpose of the Spotlight Session and how important it is to recognise and celebrate the efforts and achievements of team members. Focus on the impact it has on team morale and productivity.

Start with a round-robin:

Begin the session with a round-robin format, where each team member takes turns expressing appreciation for a colleague. Encourage specific examples of how their contributions have made a difference.

Rotate spotlight:

Without losing authenticity, try to ensure that everyone has a chance to both give and receive appreciation.

Include remote team members:

If team members work remotely, utilise video conferencing or other digital platforms to include them in the session. Ensure that everyone feels included and valued.

Document appreciation:

Keep a record of the appreciation shared during the session. This could be in the form of a shared document, a dedicated channel in the team communication platform or a physical appreciation board in the office.

Regular sessions:

Schedule regular Spotlight Sessions to ensure that recognition remains an ongoing practice within the team.

You may want to create categories for recognition linked to your desire to create a high-performing team. They could potentially be:

1. **The Extra Mile Award:** Appreciating employees who display discretionary effort when supporting their peers or customers.

(continued)

(continued)

2. **Freedom Award:** The leader who consistently empowers and gives their team autonomy.

3. **Mentorship Spotlight:** Appreciating employees who actively mentor and guide their colleagues, aiding in their professional growth and who role model integrity.

4. **Continuous Improvement:** Acknowledging employees who consistently seek ways to improve processes and operations.

5. **Knowledge Sharing:** Acknowledging employees who take time to listen to what their colleagues need and then actively share their knowledge, insights and expertise.

6. **Ownership Award**: An award for employees who have taken ownership of a specific task and driven it through to fruition.

7. **Stretch Award:** For the individual or team who has defined a clear and challenging goal and worked towards achieving that.

8. **The JFK Award:** For an individual who understands that regardless of their role, if they can do it to the best of their ability, it has an impact.

9. **Milestone Travel:** Recognising employees who have been resilient or who have achieved significant milestones or goals.

10. **Diverse and Inclusive Culture:** Rewarding employees who champion diversity and inclusion.

11. **Safety:** Acknowledging and celebrating employees who prioritise creating psychologically safe environments.

12. **One Team Ethos:** Rewarding employees who consistently embody and promote that we are all in this together.

Why It Works

Expressing gratitude fosters a sense of camaraderie and strengthens relationships within the team. Employees who feel valued and appreciated are also more likely to stay with the organisation long term.

Defined Processes Support Empowered People

Empowered people can only get so far on their own. If they don't have direction and support, they will fail to achieve collective goals no matter how strong they are as individuals. This is where defined processes come in. However, the processes we've covered in this part of the book may not have been what you were expecting.

All too often topics like recognition and communication are dismissed as 'soft'—or they certainly have been in the past. But as Yvette demonstrated, without clear communication to support your processes, you won't get very far.

Accountability and goal setting still aren't used within businesses as often as they need to be in order to truly drive high performance at every level. These processes stretch across every level of an organisation, and that's what makes them so effective. When they're done well, as Dan and Andreas highlighted, they can help everyone in an organisation to push towards excellence, both individually and as a team.

Then, we have recognition, which is often what pushes people to do more than expected. When you go the extra mile and don't even receive a 'thank you', it demotivates you. As a leader, this is hard to recover from, and it will take more than one 'thank you' to tip the scales back in your favour. Unlocking discretionary effort among everyone on your team will set them on a path to high performance and as Caoimhe showed us, often doing so doesn't cost a penny.

All of this leads us into the importance of creating a supportive culture at your organisation and the four attributes that underpin everything we've discussed so far.

Part III

Supportive Culture

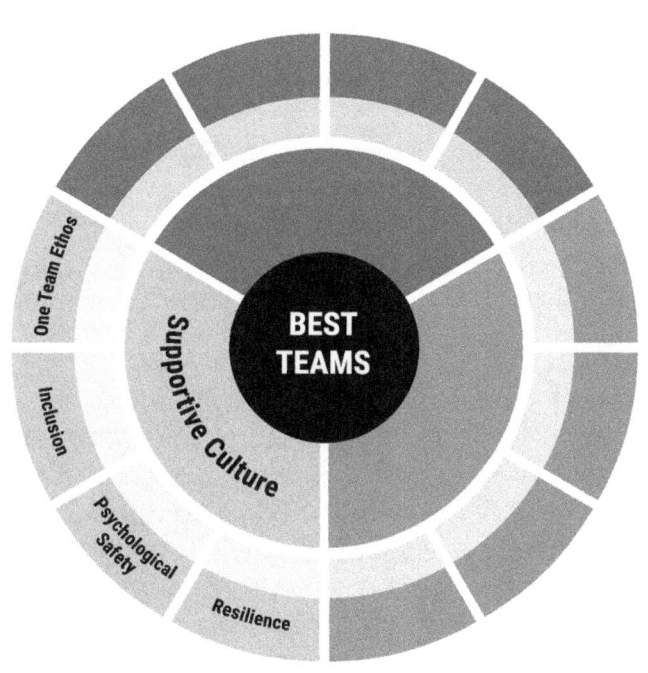

Ernest Shackleton's Imperial Trans-Antarctic Expedition of 1914–1917 faced extreme adversity during their mission to cross Antarctica, and the success of their survival is primarily attributed to the inclusive and trust-based culture Shackleton cultivated among his team, even under the harshest conditions.

Shackleton's mission began with high hopes of becoming the first to traverse the Antarctic continent. However, shortly after departure, the team's ship, the *Endurance*, became trapped in the ice, and the crew found themselves stranded in one of the most remote and unforgiving places on Earth. The ice eventually destroyed the ship, leaving Shackleton and his 27-man crew with no means of communication with the outside world, no food supply and nowhere to go.

One of Shackleton's greatest strengths as a leader was his ability to build a strong, inclusive culture despite dire circumstances. From the start, Shackleton ensured that all crew members felt involved in decision-making and understood their importance in the survival effort. He recognised his men's diverse skills and assigned roles based on their strengths, ensuring that everyone felt valuable and that no one was left behind.

Trust was crucial in these extreme conditions. Shackleton communicated openly with his team, constantly assuring them that their safety was his priority. His leadership was grounded in honesty, and he led by example. The crew trusted Shackleton not only as their leader but also as someone willing to share the hardships of the journey. His decision to remain calm and keep morale high, even when faced with seemingly insurmountable odds, played a key role in their survival.

The resilience of Shackleton and his crew was tested to the limits during the months of isolation, hunger, and hardship. Despite the constant challenges, the sense of camaraderie and mutual support among the crew never wavered. Their shared belief in each other and their leader kept them from giving up.

After months of hardship, Shackleton and a small group of men embarked on a dangerous journey to reach civilisation and organise a rescue. They managed to return to save the entire crew, and not a single life was lost during the whole ordeal.

Shackleton's expedition is widely regarded as one of the greatest survival stories in history. This is not just because of the physical challenges they overcame, but also because of the inclusive, resilient and trust-based culture that Shackleton created. His leadership taught the world that a team united by trust and mutual respect could face even the harshest of conditions and emerge victorious.

But did you spot the other common threads that we've already explored in Shackleton's story? Clear and strong communication was essential, as was recognition of what the crew were doing to support one another and ultimately stay alive. Although I very much doubt that Shackleton set goals in the sense that Andreas and I discussed, they were all working towards a higher purpose—staying alive and being rescued—and they faced the ultimate accountability: fail and you die.

Systems and processes that support empowered people will only take you so far though. What's needed to truly attain high performance, and maintain it, is a supportive culture that is built on resilience, inclusivity and psychological safety. It is these attributes that feed into a One Team Ethos, and it's here that the magic happens, as we'll explore in the chapters dedicated to the next four attributes around building a supportive culture.

11

How Resilience Impacts High-Performing Teams

On the morning of 15 January 2009, the crew of US Airways Flight 1549 didn't wake up thinking 'we must be resilient today'. However, on that day, they certainly displayed resilience. What they were clear on before they boarded the aeroplane were their roles and responsibilities and how they interlinked with the roles of others. They knew what to do if things didn't go to plan, and if something unexpected were to happen, they could respond instinctively.

And things didn't go to plan.

In what became known as the 'Miracle on the Hudson', pilot 'Sully' Sullenberger and his crew had to perform an emergency landing in the Hudson when all engine power was lost after striking a flock of birds shortly after takeoff. In an incident that lasted just three and a half minutes, Sullenberger referred to his team as being able to 'collaborate wordlessly' saving the lives of the 155 people on board.

Teams that excel at resilience demonstrate the ability to function and even thrive in a dynamic and uncertain environment. They embrace change, learn from adversity and proactively shape their future to achieve success and sustainability.

If a team doesn't have a culture of resilience, there is often a strong resistance to change, with employees and leaders reluctant to embrace new ideas, technologies or ways of working. This resistance hampers innovation and inhibits the organisation's ability to respond effectively to evolving market dynamics.

A resilient team ensures that rigid processes, hierarchies and decision-making structures that hinder flexibility and agility are removed, enabling the organisation to anticipate and prepare for potential challenges or disruptions.

When faced with unexpected events or crises how does your team respond? Does it bounce back quickly, or do you experience prolonged periods of downtime or inefficiency?

Resilient Leaders Create Resilient Organisations

IBM (International Business Machines Corporation) has consistently demonstrated resilience through its ability to reinvent itself and adapt to technological changes over its century-long history. Founded in 1911, IBM initially focused on manufacturing business machines like clocks and punch-card tabulators. By the mid-20th century, it became a global computing leader, dominating the market with its mainframe systems, notably the System/360, which revolutionised enterprise computing.

However, the rise of personal computers in the 1980s and 1990s challenged IBM's business model. Although it was instrumental in developing the IBM PC, the decision to licence its PC architecture allowed competitors like Dell and HP to flourish, leading to a decline in IBM's PC market share. This was a period of financial strain for the company, but IBM's resilience emerged through a transformative pivot under CEO Lou Gerstner in 1993. Gerstner recognised the shift from hardware to services, repositioning IBM as an IT consulting and solutions company. This helped IBM regain stability and laid the foundation for its future.

In 2005, IBM sold its PC division to Lenovo, marking a decisive shift away from hardware. This allowed IBM to focus on software, IT services and emerging fields like artificial intelligence and cloud computing. The next major step in IBM's transformation came in 2019 with its $34 billion acquisition of Red Hat, a leading open-source software provider. Red Hat is best known for its enterprise operating system, Red Hat Enterprise Linux, as well as its contributions to cloud-native technologies such as containers and Kubernetes.

This acquisition was significant for IBM's strategy in multiple ways. Red Hat brought a robust portfolio in open-source and hybrid cloud technologies, helping IBM compete more effectively with cloud giants like Amazon Web Services, Microsoft Azure and Google Cloud. The acquisition positioned IBM to offer flexible hybrid cloud solutions, leveraging Red Hat's technology to bridge on-premises data centres with public cloud environments. IBM's hybrid cloud approach became a central pillar of its strategy, as more enterprises sought flexibility to deploy workloads across multiple cloud and on-premises environments.

Through its acquisition of Red Hat, IBM demonstrated resilience by aligning with the cloud and open-source trends that dominate today's digital landscape. This strategic acquisition underscores IBM's commitment to staying relevant and competitive as it continues to innovate and adapt to meet the evolving needs of modern enterprises.

As Lou Gerstner said, 'No institution will go through fundamental change unless it believes it is in deep trouble and needs to do something different to survive'.[1] When you as a leader, and your organisation, are resilient, you are more likely to be able to find your way out of those troubled times and pivot towards a brighter future.

In fact, resilient leaders are essential because they lead the way when it comes to developing organisational resilience. They show everyone else how to become more resilient, and demonstrate the impact that this resilience can have on a business.

It's perhaps no surprise, given the rate of change in this sector, that my next example of resilience also comes from the tech world. But this time the focus is on the impact a resilient leader can have on a business. Steve Jobs demonstrated resilience through his ability to overcome setbacks and use each challenge as a springboard for innovation, which had a profound and transformative impact on Apple.

Jobs demonstrated resilience at many points during his career, not just when he was at the helm of Apple. In fact, one example of his resilience came in 1985 when he was ousted from Apple, the company he co-founded.

Rather than giving up, he used this setback as an opportunity to pursue other ventures. He founded NeXT, a computer platform development company, and invested in Pixar Animation Studios, where he helped revolutionise animated films. NeXT eventually caught the attention of

Apple in the mid-1990s when Apple was struggling with declining sales and limited innovation. In 1997, Apple acquired NeXT, bringing Jobs back into the company, this time as CEO.

Upon his return, Jobs was faced with the enormous challenge of turning around a company that was on the brink of bankruptcy. He immediately demonstrated resilience by making tough decisions that would refocus Apple's mission. He cut underperforming product lines, streamlined the company's offerings and emphasised simplicity and design in its products. Jobs had a clear vision for Apple, focusing on innovation and user experience, which was evident in the release of revolutionary products like the iMac, iPod, iPhone and iPad. These products were not only technologically advanced but also emphasised design, transforming Apple into one of the most valuable and respected brands in the world.

Jobs' resilience also impacted Apple's culture. He instilled a culture of high expectations and innovation, encouraging employees to 'think different' and take risks. This led to a series of groundbreaking products that set industry standards and built Apple's reputation for quality and innovation. Under Jobs' leadership, Apple became a symbol of resilience itself, adapting to shifts in technology and consistently setting trends in the tech industry.

Both Gerstner and Jobs led their organisations through periods of significant change by adapting to their changed circumstances. How often do you make time to check in on what's happening within your industry? Could you encourage everyone on your team to take some time to identify changes in your industry and discuss how you can adapt to not only survive them, but thrive?

In Conversation With Noelle Perkins, Executive Vice President, General Counsel & Corporate Secretary, Cushman & Wakefield

All of us experienced the need for resilience during the COVID-19 pandemic in 2020, but for a century-old business like Cushman & Wakefield, this was just one more in a long line of challenges to navigate. I spoke to the organisation's Executive Vice President, General Counsel & Corporate Secretary Noelle Perkins about how to build our individual and team resilience to create resilient organisations.

MARC: *How important is resilience within your business?*

NOELLE: Incredibly important. In fact, so important that when we launched our new brand and values platform in 2024, 'resilient' became one of our core values. Necessity is the mother of invention, and we are in a cyclical industry. A lot of what we do depends on the macro-economic situation, especially interest rates. This means we must be prepared to operate through that cycle, regardless of whether interest rates are low or high, business is booming or sluggish.

MARC: *And what is it about your business that makes you think it is resilient?*

NOELLE: The company is more than 100 years old, which shows resilience in itself. We were responsible for overseeing the development of the United Nations Complex in New York in 1946 and were project developer for the Sears Tower in Chicago in 1969. We took the company public in 2018 and we were a leading industry voice through COVID-19. A lot has changed in the built environment in that time. But the organisation has survived because it has adapted.

Take what's happened since 2019 as an example. In 2019, the industry was at the peak of the cycle. We were very focused on office leasing and brokerage. But then in 2020, COVID-19 hit. Suddenly, nobody went to the office anymore. What sustained us at that time was the services side of our business—we provided clean, safe and secure places. The ability to offset a challenging economic environment is a cornerstone of resilience.

Since the pandemic, we have faced a period of decades-high interest rates, the likes of which we haven't seen since the 1970s and early 1980s. And as interest rates gradually come down, transactions will return, which will be great for us. As a business, we plan for all parts of the cycle.

MARC: *What does it look like day to day when a team or an individual is being resilient?*

NOELLE: Being resilient means leaning on different people in different groups at different times. From a business perspective, it's the ability to lean on volatility in the good times and predictability in the harder times. What makes our business resilient is having a diversified bench that can respond and show strength in different situations.

From an individual perspective, we need leaders to be wired in such a way that they can withstand the ups and downs. What does that look like? Never getting too high on the highs or too low on the lows—being able to see the bigger, longer picture regardless of what is happening in any given moment. I think the other thing that is important from an individual perspective is a sense of team. What I mean by this is a sense that we cannot execute well if we don't band together, build off of one another and act with an enterprise mindset.

MARC: *So, thinking about how we're all wired differently and how we cope in challenging times varies. What can a team, or organisation, do to accept that we're all different and we can't all cope in the same way?*

NOELLE: I think it does go back to recognising what you just said, which is 'we are all different', and that is what makes us perfect when you put us all together. You will have people who are very comfortable staying right in that middle space, not too high during the peaks, not too low during the valleys. Some thrive on the highs. We know those people. We love those people. They are great when it's great. Then, there are those people who are just fantastic in a crisis, and they save you during the tough times. Frankly, sometimes those folks have a hard time operating when there isn't a crisis! When you bring all of those people together, you can do anything.

MARC: *Your team supports various elements of the business. What do you tend to see when a team is struggling from a resilience point of view?*

NOELLE: You'll see a 'me-first' attitude for starters. You'll see a lack of interconnectedness, which is maybe another representation of a me-first attitude. You'll see things getting in the way of what should matter. Instead of being focused on the performance tactics, and the things that are going to help you perform, you'll see people getting distracted. That could be office politics, individual performance or any number of other factors.

It's fascinating because, in life, the way you succeed initially is often due to your individual performance. That's what gets someone noticed and that's what can attract developmental investment. But there comes a point when that individual high performer must pivot and recognise that it's no longer about your performance—it's about how you help others perform. It's about something much bigger than yourself. Lots of people have said this in lots of different ways—'What Got You Here Won't Get You There'—but it is true. You initially advance on your individual successes, but no matter how great you are, you can't go as far as a high-performing team.

MARC: *How do you develop resilience within your own team?*

NOELLE: One thing that we needed to do was better leverage technology. Technology is efficient, and it takes waste out of the system. It also eliminates the mundane. So, the more you leverage technology, the more you can focus on what really matters and get things done better and faster. Luckily, we have an awesome technology team and they have been great to partner with on this front.

For my team specifically, we moved from a subject matter expert model to a generalist model. In tough times, I'm not sure that you have the luxury of being a specialist. All of us have to be willing to keep learning, adapt, and take on something that is not totally comfortable. That's okay—that's how we evolve and get closer to the business, embedding ourselves more deeply, making it more seamless.

There is no better way to advise than from within. If you are in a position where you are expected to give counsel and you're sitting externally, you can do it and you'll spot the big things. But because there's distance, you won't be able to spot the little things, because you aren't integrated in a meaningful way. The aim is making sure that you have the right shape of team with the right individuals.

MARC: *What were the technological changes you made?*

NOELLE: One was E-billing. Gone are the days when someone had to manually review a paper invoice. Another was managing deadlines on lawsuits. We leverage workflow management for contracts. In the olden days, someone would review a contract, make changes, have questions and then email it around to all the different people in the company. It would probably take days, or even weeks. It was very inefficient. Now, all that activity is routed through a system where the full history of what has happened is captured in the system. You can easily delegate tasks and have different people working on it at the same time.

More broadly, in that same system, we're working to optimise revenue capture. We want to be sure that we are invoicing for all of the work we do and not let little things slip through the cracks. That's a level of operational rigor that is enabled through technology. And, frankly, it helps build resilience.

MARC: *Can we talk a little bit about when you're leading a team? Some things are within your control. Some things are out of your control. Some are internal to the business, and some things are external. Can you share your thoughts on the challenges leaders face?*

NOELLE: This will be glaringly obvious, but you do have to recognise those things over which you do not have control and let go. I would advise not wasting energy on trying to manipulate or control those things. Step one is, therefore, to focus on what you absolutely can control.

A lot of times you are faced with really difficult decisions, and you have to decide: Am I going to go left, or am I going to go right? I think data and information is the best cure to a bad decision. If you're going to make decisions about things that are difficult, about things that you can control or influence, I would suggest that you do that from an extremely informed perspective.

MARC: *How do you personally stay resilient?*

NOELLE: That's a deep question! It starts with an understanding of your personal purpose. From there, it is an understanding of what you're good at and what motivates you. What are the things that you need to watch out for and manage within yourself? Self-awareness is crucial. Speaking as a full-time working mom, finding balance is tough. There are trade-offs.

If you looked at a pie chart of my time allocation this week, it would be more allocated towards work. I am traveling and am physically not with my children. This weekend, the pie chart will look much different. There will be a tiny sliver that is allocated to work, with much more allocated to my children, exercise and my friends. If someone were to look at the pie chart of my weekend, they would say, 'Wow, she doesn't take her work very seriously'. If they looked at my pie chart for this week, they would say, 'Well, she's not a very good mom. She doesn't really spend that much time with her kids, does she?' At any given time, the pie chart is not balanced, but if you aggregate it over time, I am a very good mother and I am also very good at my job. That is how you do it, in my opinion.

You just have to lean in on different things at different times and let it all even out. You have to have a piece of you that is very career focused, a piece of you that, at least for me, is parent focused, a piece that is focused on wellbeing, etc. Somewhere I heard about the acronym SPIRE, which suggests some areas to focus on to achieve balance: Spiritual, Physical, Intellectual, Relational and Emotional. The idea is that you figure out a way to have all those things feature in your life in some form, and doing so is a pathway to being resilient and fulfilled.

MARC: *When you're talking with people who are earlier on in their career, what advice are you giving them?*

NOELLE: I try to make people feel like it's okay to have your pie chart look different at different times. In other words, if you're not at your desk at 7pm, that does not mean that you are not a hard worker or committed. I want to liberate people from this idea that they must prove something external or cosmetic. The way you demonstrate your work ethic or your contribution is in the work itself. I try to model this by working hard at doing the job, but having appropriate boundaries. I will not apologise for the fact that I leave at 4:30pm to catch my train. That is what I do to be home in time to help my kids with their homework in the evening. But I also start my day quite early, so by 4:30pm I'm in a position to pivot my energies.

In the past, I worried about people saying, 'Oh, she's leaving at 4:30pm, she must not be focused on her career'. That's not true, but I'm less worried about what people think—what matters to me is the work, getting it done and getting it done well. If I'm sitting at the office until 9pm, but I'm telling everyone else, 'It's okay, you can set boundaries', I'm not sure it would resonate with people because my words and actions wouldn't match.

I also talk about my kids and share the fact that I am a working mom. I used to hide that. I think a lot of women have at various points in their careers. Then, the pandemic happened, and everybody's lives were on full display for everyone, which was a good thing in many ways even though it didn't seem that way at the time. Now, I'm trying to do my part to make it an obvious reality that is neither good nor bad, just real.

MARC: *Any final thoughts on resilience?*

NOELLE: I'm looking at your Best Teams Model, and there is something about the interconnectedness of the attributes that really speaks to this topic. All of these attributes contribute to building your resilience. Resilience, if you think about it, is having the ability to absorb, buffer and survive, and you get that by doing many of those other things in the model.

Noelle and I covered a lot of ground in our conversation. Here are my top three takeaways from our discussion:

1. *To develop a resilient organisation, you need to diversify your offering so that you can offset and support divisions that are facing challenges that may not be of their making.*

2. *A resilient team is made up of many different individuals, some of whom are great at celebrating the wins, others who are fantastic in a crisis and others who sit in the middle. Don't underestimate the value of the steady performers who stay grounded throughout the highs and the lows.*

3. *Individually, being resilient means finding the right balance within your life. But you don't need to have the perfect balance every day. The key is ensuring every part of your life balances in the long term.*

As Noelle identified, there is no single thing that builds resilience, either individually, in a team or in an organisation. Resilience comes from a wide range of attributes and actions. That made choosing a single exercise to support resilience quite a challenge, but I've decided to focus on building trust. Trust is essential not only for the attribute of resilience, but for every attribute that makes up the Best Teams Model. And it is especially important for creating a supportive culture.

Leaders as Coach

Understanding the three interconnecting types of resilience is important for any leader. They are organisational, team and individual resilience, and each contributes to overall adaptability and performance.

Organisational resilience refers to a company's ability to respond to crises, adapt to change and sustain long-term success. It involves strong leadership, a supportive culture and flexible structures. (Think IBM).

Individual resilience is each person's ability to handle stress and setbacks, fostered by self-awareness, adaptability and optimism. (Look at Steve Jobs).

Team resilience is the collective capacity of a group to overcome challenges, relying on trust, communication and shared goals. It's strengthened by a positive environment and mutual support. (Perfectly demonstrated by the crew of Flight 1549).

This book focuses on team performance, and I have dedicated specific chapters to communication and shared goals, so I'd like to focus on trust for this Leader as Coach section. Trust is also integral to psychological safety, which we will explore in the next chapter.

(continued)

(continued)

Process

The exercise I want to share here is called 'Two Truths and a Dream'. You may well have played 'Two Truths and a Lie'—a game that has been around for centuries. Substituting the lie with a dream gives us an opportunity to better know the aspirations of a colleague.

Objective: Build trust by encouraging team members to share personal truths and aspirations, fostering authenticity, understanding and connection.

Purpose: Explain that this activity is designed to help the team connect on a deeper level by sharing real aspects of themselves and their dreams for the future.

Ground rules:
- Listen actively and without judgment.

- Respect everyone's privacy—don't pressure anyone to share more than they're comfortable with.

Sharing and guessing:
1. Each participant shares three statements:
2. Two truths about themselves—interesting, unique or meaningful facts.
3. One dream—a personal or professional aspiration they hope to achieve.

You will want to keep them all in the same tense, or it will be obvious which one is the dream.

For example, keeping everything in the past tense, mine could be:

- *I have piloted a helicopter.*
- *I was an extra in the film* Gladiator.
- *I have chaired an organisation.*

Once a person has shared their three statements with the group, the rest of the group guesses which of the three is their dream.

After making guesses, the speaker reveals which statements are the truths and which is the dream. Take a moment for the person to elaborate on their dream and share why it's important to them. Repeat the process until everyone has had a turn.

So, from my statements, my dream is to fly a helicopter. This is because my father was a winchman on an air/sea helicopter, and he always spoke so positively about the work he did.

Reflection and discussion:

After everyone has shared, facilitate a group discussion using prompts such as:

- 'What did you learn about your teammates that you didn't know before?'

- 'Were there any dreams that resonated with or inspired you?'
- 'How can we as a team support each other's dreams?'

Highlight how understanding each other's stories and aspirations strengthens trust and connection.

(continued)

(continued)

Why It Works

- *Personal disclosure:* Sharing truths helps people reveal authentic parts of themselves, building trust.

- *Shared aspirations:* Discussing dreams humanises team members and fosters mutual encouragement.

- *Engaging and fun:* The guessing element creates a light-hearted and interactive environment, making the activity enjoyable while still meaningful.

'Two Truths and a Dream' is an engaging way to build trust by balancing vulnerability with fun, leaving the team feeling more connected and inspired, and therefore more resilient to challenges they may face.

12

The Role of Psychological Safety in High-Performing Teams

In 2012, Google was on a mission. They wanted to build the perfect team, and they were willing to invest the time required to understand what it took. So, they embarked on a project. They gave it the code name 'Aristotle' because of his quote, 'The whole is greater than the sum of its parts'. Two years later, after analysing 180 different teams, they were able to distil their findings to one attribute that impacted team performance more than any other: psychological safety.

Harvard Business School Professor Amy Edmondson coined the term 'team psychological safety' in the 1990s to describe work environments where candour is expected and where employees can speak up without fear of retribution.

Teams that create psychologically safe and trusting environments enable a positive work environment where employees feel valued, respected and empowered to contribute their best work. This fosters a culture of collaboration, innovation, and continuous improvement, driving organisational success and resilience.

In this kind of environment, employees are also encouraged to learn from mistakes. We heard from Simon in Chapter 6 about how embracing mistakes and learning from them is central to Microsoft's culture. This again demonstrates the interconnected nature of all of these attributes. Having a growth mindset contributes to creating psychological safety within teams and organisations.

When there isn't psychological safety, employees hesitate to voice their opinions, ideas or concerns for fear of criticism, ridicule or retaliation. This contributes to higher levels of stress and burnout among employees, as they may feel constant pressure to perform without adequate support or recognition. Psychological safety is essential for building strong working relationships and effective communication.

You will instinctively know if your team has psychological safety. Ask yourself does everyone, regardless of hierarchy, feel able to contribute freely? Or do you see people get shot down for voicing an opinion which is unwelcome?

What Does Psychological Safety Look Like?

Prioritising psychological safety is essential for organisations aiming to create an environment where employees can innovate, collaborate and express ideas openly without fear of backlash. This atmosphere is critical for fostering creativity, well-being and problem-solving, as it allows team members to feel confident in taking risks, sharing thoughts and addressing issues openly. Psychological safety not only leads to higher engagement and productivity but also promotes personal growth and builds strong team dynamics.

Here's how Pixar, Shopify and Atlassian embody psychological safety and the positive outcomes it brings to their workplace cultures. Each organisation has taken a different approach, and each is equally valid.

Fostering Psychological Safety Through Creative Collaboration

Pixar is renowned for its focus on creativity, which is nurtured through a psychologically safe environment where employees can voice their opinions freely. A key feature of Pixar's culture is its 'Braintrust' meetings, where teams come together to provide constructive feedback on ongoing projects. In these meetings, every team member, regardless of rank, can offer insights and criticisms to improve the work, making each employee's perspective valuable and heard.

This open forum encourages feedback that is honest yet respectful, helping employees feel comfortable with vulnerability. By fostering such an environment, Pixar not only enhances creative output but also builds trust and collaboration among employees. Team members know they are in a space where failure and experimentation are accepted, which is essential for creativity and innovation to flourish.

This practice at Pixar exemplifies the concept of 'learning through failure' by giving employees the freedom to try new approaches without the fear of punitive consequences if things don't go as planned. Pixar's approach has helped establish a feedback-rich culture that values continuous improvement, resilience and collaboration, ultimately resulting in high-quality creative content that resonates with audiences worldwide.

Promoting Psychological Safety Through Mental Health Support

Shopify, a global e-commerce platform, places a strong emphasis on employee well-being as a foundation for psychological safety. The company's commitment to mental health is demonstrated through various support programs, including counselling services, mindfulness resources and open dialogue initiatives. Shopify has established an environment where employees feel encouraged to discuss mental health challenges, reducing the stigma around mental well-being in the workplace.

By normalising conversations around mental health, Shopify creates a supportive culture where employees can openly address personal struggles that may impact their work. This approach not only shows empathy but also reinforces trust and psychological safety within the organisation. When employees feel supported, they are more likely to engage fully and contribute their best efforts, leading to higher productivity and job satisfaction. Shopify's emphasis on mental health sends a clear message: the company values employees' holistic well-being. This support translates into a more resilient and engaged workforce.

In addition to formal resources, Shopify's inclusive and supportive culture is reinforced through policies and programs that promote work–life balance, such as flexible scheduling and remote work options. This approach to psychological safety, which includes mental, emotional and logistical support, helps foster an environment where employees feel valued and safe to express themselves.

Building Psychological Safety Through Team Collaboration

Atlassian, a global software company, promotes psychological safety through a team-oriented culture that emphasises transparency and collaboration. Known for its popular project management tools like Jira and Trello, Atlassian also champions 'Team Playbook' and 'Health Monitors'—resources specifically designed to facilitate open communication and build trust among team members. The 'Team Playbook' includes exercises and practices that encourage honest conversations and improve team dynamics, while 'Health Monitors' help teams assess their effectiveness and identify areas for improvement.

In these sessions, team members can openly discuss any challenges, concerns or barriers they are facing. Atlassian encourages employees to speak up about issues or concerns without fear of retribution, reinforcing a culture where each individual's voice is respected. This open communication fosters trust and psychological safety, creating a work environment where employees can address issues candidly and seek solutions collaboratively. By providing structured tools to support communication and feedback, Atlassian empowers teams to own their development, making psychological safety an integral part of their operations.

Additionally, Atlassian's focus on continuous learning and development supports psychological safety by ensuring that employees have the resources to grow and improve. Regular feedback sessions and goal-setting processes allow employees to understand their strengths and areas for growth, building a culture that values progress and learning over perfection. This open approach to development creates an environment where employees feel empowered to take risks and learn from mistakes, driving both individual and organisational growth.

One element that all of these examples share is openness, whether that's in how people communicate with one another, how the business communicates with its employees, or being able to be open about mistakes and what you learned from them. Take a moment now to consider if you could be more open as a team. Can you take inspiration from one of these examples to introduce more candid and open discussions into your day-to-day team interactions?

The Impact of Psychological Safety

By prioritising psychological safety, companies like Pixar, Shopify and Atlassian create work environments where employees feel supported, valued and motivated to contribute meaningfully. Psychological safety fosters a culture where innovation can thrive, as employees are more likely to take creative risks when they feel secure. It also leads to better teamwork, as open communication and trust allow teams to navigate challenges collaboratively and support each other's growth.

In Conversation with Andria Vidler, CEO of Allwyn

Andria Vidler is CEO of Allwyn UK, the operator for the UK's National Lottery and employer of 2,000 people across the country. The organisation generates over £7 billion in sales, which not only funds the prizes available, but also a range of good causes. At the start of our discussion, Andria told me that she isn't an 'expert' in psychological safety, but what she shared highlights how if you get the foundations right, intentionally or otherwise, psychological safety will follow.

MARC: *What kind of environment do you aim to create for your 2,000 employees? Can you describe the culture?*

ANDRIA: I come from a background of working with creative talent, whether that's been at the BBC, Capital Radio, magazines, or music at EMI; my whole background has been working with talent-led organisations. In my experience, creative individuals perform at their best when they believe they are really giving their best, and that requires clarity on brief and role. It also requires making them feel empowered.

For instance, if you want to get the best out of a musical artist, you don't nag them every day. You give them the space to breathe and work on their own, but you also give them a really clear brief. That's also true of a journalist who's writing a newspaper article or investigating something for a news programme. In fact, it's true in most creative roles. So, you need to set a framework that they feel comfortable in and that allows them to perform at their best. If you have an organisation where everyone is performing at their best level, the aggregate is working at its very best.

When I think about creating the perfect environment in these organisations that I lead,

I want to create an organisation where everyone knows the destination. They understand the goal that we need to achieve, why we're trying to achieve it, and their role in that team.

Once you've established this understanding, you give them clear deadlines and parameters. You tell them what they can make a decision on and what they need to come back to you for. Often, the need for someone on the team to seek approval or agreement is so that they aren't overexposed. You're providing air cover for them and ensuring that they feel safe to act within the parameters of their role. An individual who's left to spend a million pounds without any checks and then spends it badly is going to have a real knock of confidence going forward. So many of the checks and balances are in place to enable growth, enable learning, and to enable people to take the right steps gradually, as opposed to being exposed to high-risk scenarios and experiencing failure in a negative way.

I like that wonderful analogy of geese all flying together. They know the country they are trying to fly to—their destination—and one goose leads. If one gets tired, they move further back in the formation, but they all continue in that V shape, because that V enables them all to get the best output. They're not all racing against the wind, at the same level, as individuals. They're all flying in the same direction and supporting one another. That is the ideal environment for me. The challenge as the leader is that it's so rare that you will have everybody that you want and the perfect person in the perfect role.

I worked at the BBC for seven and a half years. We achieved a lot and I learnt even more. Within that time, there was a special period of four months where I believe my direct colleagues and team were all working brilliantly together. We were all clear about our roles and how all the cogs worked well together. There was a high level of trust between everyone on the team, which meant we felt psychologically safe working together. That safety meant we individually and collectively felt more confident about how to push each other further and challenge how we could outperform further. Then someone on the team got pregnant and unsurprisingly took maternity leave. Whilst we were all very happy for them, the new person who came in understandably couldn't fly at the same pace as the rest of us and had none of the same intuition. As a team, that psychological safety had been disrupted. We didn't trust every other person in exactly the same way. The environment subtly shifted and things felt a little off. When that happens, and it always will at some point in any team, you have to start again and strive to get to as near to this harmony as possible.

MARC: *I like the analogies you've used there and I guess you are head goose!*

ANDRIA: Yes, but sometimes I need to rest and let somebody else on a particular project lead, and I tuck in behind. Recognising that, and trusting someone else on the team to step up and lead for a while, is a good sign that we have psychological safety within our team.

MARC: *You mentioned setting parameters is crucial. Is part of the mix then trusting people and giving them the space to make their own decisions and to have opinions?*

ANDRIA: The most important part of trust is actually the trust between individuals, rather than an individual being trusted to always deliver. It takes time to trust everybody equally, because new people come into teams, some people know each other, some people don't know each other. It's ever changing. So, I think an important part of a high-performing team is learning that people are people and not their role. To create true psychological safety, you need to trust each person on the team on a personal level.

As an example, I have just recruited a new head of security, and my level of trust in his ability to do the role is high. I believe he is the best person for the job, but nobody else knows him and we don't really know how he likes to work yet. So, you might trust someone from a role's perspective but you don't necessarily trust they're going to communicate everything the same way you want it to be communicated. That takes time. Of course you need to trust their ability to do the job, but you also need to allow time and space for that personal level of trust to develop not just between you and any new team members, but between everyone on your team.

I also strongly believe in the benefit of having differing opinions. Spending seven years at the BBC and working mostly with news journalists was fantastic, because it really educated me on the benefits of a difference of opinion. Playing devil's advocate is not about getting in the way. You do it to improve something. I love the fact that the news journalists at the BBC tested each other beyond belief to ensure that up until the last minute before they went live for the *Six O'Clock* or *Nine O'Clock News*, they would be improving the way they presented things. They tested each other constantly to try and improve.

Being able to test one another in a constructive way requires trust though. Without trust, it can feel confrontational, which means people may not feel safe sharing opposing views.

This brings us back to everyone understanding our direction of travel. Learning to trust each other is about agreeing on the destination we're heading to. So, if my new head of security doesn't know where we're heading as an organisation and a team, he could improve security so much that I can't play our games and I can't work because my laptop is locked down to prevent cyberattacks. He might be performing his role, but if he goes too far, he isn't working for the good of the team. To prevent this kind of narrow focus, he has to be aligned with the team's overall ambition. He has to be able to work with the gaming developers. He has to be able to work with the marketers.

He has to be able to work with retailers to ensure that our platform is as safe as it can be, enabling as many people to play as possible. Everybody has to be aligned to the overarching goal.

You cannot always anticipate what's coming, so you always have to adapt, but your destination stays the same. Everyone knows we are flying in that direction, and we need to land by that time. Therefore, you have to overcome the hurdles and build trust so that we've all got each other's backs. We will help each other to get there, and we will celebrate when someone does a great job and we get a bit of the way to our destination. Trust on a team and individual level is crucial for creating an environment that feels psychologically safe and allows people to do their best work.

MARC: *How do you then bring a new person in and make sure that they adopt the right behaviours?*

ANDRIA: We've introduced some team Rules of Engagement. These cover things like How urgent is it if I WhatsApp? When can I email? When can I call? What's normal, and what's an emergency? It's also important to understand a person as an individual. I foolishly land in jobs that often need a lot of change and need people to be working at breakneck speed very quickly, so I have to find ways of building that trust and psychological safety without holding up the work we have to do. As a result, I tend to focus time together in two ways. One is to acknowledge that although this is a business problem that we're trying to resolve together, we can also get to know each other a bit better at the same time. I might get everyone to bring a photograph in, and ask them to describe why that photograph is important to them. What's the memory? What's the importance of the people in it? Or it could be a simple question like, what's your favourite song and why?

Sometimes I might get everyone to write something on a Post-It note at the start of a meeting, and put them in a hat. Then after a break I pull a couple out and say, 'Guess who?' These are quick little things you can do around the table, which bring alive someone's background, someone's story, and it often reveals their passions, interests and hobbies. It's really important to build those connections around the team because personal connections accelerate a team's bonding process and make everyone feel more comfortable more quickly. But doing this is not easy.

MARC: *People often say your culture is only as good as the worst behaviour that you're willing to walk past and ignore. Can you share examples of where you will step in to improve psychological safety to enable people to be themselves and deliver to the best of their ability?*

ANDRIA: We've just done a town hall where the executives on a panel were quizzed by an employee. They talked about what they expect of each other, what they expect of the teams and what the team should expect of them. It was very open and very transparent. I think clarity really helps when it comes to establishing psychological safety. It's hard to call out bad behaviour if you're not clear about what good looks like.

I also ask the team what they hate about my behaviour, and they tell me! Often their feedback for me is that because I'm too impatient and I want things to move faster, in my ambition to help them get to the answer quickly, I interrupt them. It's a really bad habit. It's one I'm aware of, so I call it out and say, 'I will not speak until you are finished'. But I know what I'm like and they now know what I'm like, and because we have had those open conversations, my behaviour can be called out without it becoming a tension point. That's a big green flag for psychological safety.

MARC: *What advice would you give to leaders who want to improve psychological safety within their team?*

ANDRIA: My advice is to focus on the things we have discussed clarity, simple rules of engagement, genuine buy-in for the destination, defined time frames, everybody pointing in the same direction. This builds momentum. If you're getting better momentum, people become braver about sharing new ideas.

I believe everyone wakes up every morning and wants to do a good job. There are very few people in this world who wake up and go, 'What can I screw up today?' In my experience, people copy success wherever they can, because they want to be successful too. So if you show them what good looks like, whether that's how you write a presentation, how you write a letter, or how you show up to a meeting, if people know what good is, people will tend to copy that because they don't want to be bad. So, the clearer you can be about expectations, the better. This creates an environment where people are braver about putting their hands up with more proactive suggestions on ways to fly faster, which is what psychological safety is all about.

MARC: *You have shared how you sometimes jump in during conversations. Do you sometimes reflect that you might not have heard from everybody in the room or do you consciously make sure that you're hearing everybody's point of view?*

ANDRIA: It's really important to find the right balance for the situation. I have inherited teams where no decisions were made unless everybody had bought in. But that did not create agility. Everything was delayed because getting everyone in a room would take time and there was not enough agility to deal with the current market challenges. The challenge became enabling the experts to run with enough empowerment, whilst keeping everyone up to speed. In a meeting where everyone is being updated, but there are really only two decision makers on this particular project, it isn't for everyone to pile in and find reasons why this cannot go ahead.

I've been in other situations, though, where you absolutely need to deliberately hear from everyone. As a leader, sometimes the most powerful impact you can have is not to say anything. I really believe that diversity is an enabler for innovation. People coming at the same problem with different experience and different perspectives is vital, and that is very much a creative industries legacy of mine. I've only known that way of working and when you get that right and everyone feels safe to share their perspectives, you get breakthrough ideas.

But you need to work out what the balance is. I'll give you an example from EMI. When I walked in the door, the direction of travel was dictated by the A and R teams (Artists and Repertoire), who were only focused on sales of records, of albums really, and a single release was there to help drive album sales. By bringing in the perspectives from other parts of the business we switched the team's mindset to create a long-lasting career for the artist. That meant we viewed the artist as a brand and a future business. When that's your perspective, it's much easier to say, 'Okay, it's not just about a single leading to an album'. You start to think more creatively as a team. For example, we built brand partnerships that generated revenue. We signed Tinie Tempah and Professor Green, and in their first year, they made more money from doing other things. This took the pressure off their writing, which enabled their first albums to be amazing successes, because we didn't rush it. Getting everyone to buy into that destination meant I could put more pressure on other parts of the organisation to really deliver much earlier on.

But we wouldn't have been able to get that buy-in if there hadn't been trust within the team, and an understanding that open and honest discussions are necessary to find the best way forward for everyone. To me, those are the foundations for psychological safety.

What I found fascinating about my conversation with Andria is that many strong leaders already take steps to create psychological safety in their teams, even if they don't use that terminology. Here are my top three takeaways from our conversation:

1. *Having a collective destination that the team is working towards, along with frameworks and clear parameters to work within, is crucial for creating a sense of safety and support among every member of a team.*

2. *Cultivating trust and bonding on a personal level is vital if you want everyone to feel safe to speak up. Teams evolve as people leave and new people come in. As a leader, you need to find a way to keep renewing the trust and bonds between your team members to maintain psychological safety for everyone on the team.*

3. *Being open to feedback—even if it's not positive—and having the humility to accept this as a leader or team member is crucial for creating psychological safety. This enhances a culture whereby everyone is encouraged to learn from their mistakes.*

Andria touched on the need to be able to accept feedback in our interview as a key marker of psychological safety. She also spoke about how important open communication has been in helping her to moderate her behaviour to enhance collaboration within her team. But embracing feedback, and ensuring that everyone feels comfortable to call out unhelpful behaviours in a constructive way, can be a challenge. Finding the right balance in how you communicate with one another is essential.

Leader as Coach

Psychological safety is essential for high-performing teams, enabling members to take risks, learn from mistakes and communicate openly, ultimately fostering innovation and productivity.

The team-building activity I like to use as a precursor to discussing and enhancing psychological safety uses the concept of radical candour to encourage honest feedback and build trust among team members. Inspired by the Radical Candor Framework by Kim Scott,[1] this exercise helps create a culture where individuals feel safe to express their thoughts openly, address issues directly and share constructive criticism without fear of negative repercussions.

Process

Preparation and Setup

When conducting a radical candour exercise with a group, it is essential to create an environment where team members feel comfortable. There are videos you can share with your team to watch online as pre-work that clearly define the concept. I start by discussing the core principles of the Radical Candor Framework, which require people to 'care personally and challenge directly'. Showing genuine concern for others while being honest improves communication and builds trust by encouraging honest conversations.

Create Ground Rules and Set Intentions

Begin by establishing ground rules to ensure that feedback remains respectful and constructive. These should include listening without interruption, avoiding defensive responses and aiming for empathy. Emphasise that the feedback should come from a place of care rather than criticism.

Encourage Self-reflection

Ask each team member to reflect on their own behaviours, communication style, and how they may impact others on the team. This step helps individuals become more aware of their strengths and areas where they could improve. Reflection can also include thinking about how they handle feedback from others and any past experiences with difficult conversations.

Introduce the 'Radical Candor Pairing'

Pair team members up and give them 10–15 minutes each to provide honest feedback to each other. The feedback should address both positive aspects ('What you do well that benefits the team') and areas for improvement ('What you could do differently to strengthen the team'). Encourage them to follow the Radical Candor model by balancing care with directness in their feedback.

Group Debrief

After everyone has shared feedback in pairs, come back together as a group. Each person can share insights they gained during the exercise without revealing confidential details from their pairing. This debrief allows the team to discuss the experience, share lessons learned, and identify any common themes in the feedback that can help the team grow collectively.

Follow-up and Commitment to Growth

Conclude the exercise by encouraging each person to set specific, actionable goals based on their feedback. Finally, encourage

(continued)

(continued)

everyone to give 'permission' to be approached for radical candour conversations within the day-to-day operation of the business.

Why It Works

This Radical Candor exercise promotes psychological safety by normalising honest feedback and demonstrating that open communication is welcomed and valued. It encourages team members to express their thoughts and concerns without fear of judgment, reducing the anxiety often associated with speaking up. Trust deepens when individuals see that they can give and receive feedback without damaging relationships, and a culture of mutual respect is strengthened.

What tends to happen after this exercise has been delivered is that people will start interactions with 'Can we have a radical candour conversation?' In doing this, they remind themselves and their colleagues of the need to be caring and direct.

Creating psychological safety within a team doesn't happen overnight, but exercises like the Radical Candor Framework provide a structured, effective way to foster it. When practised consistently, this exercise can transform team dynamics by building a foundation of trust, open communication and respect.

13

The Impact
of Inclusion on
High-Performing Teams

Inclusion naturally follows on from psychological safety, because you can't have one without the other. It is a crucial attribute for creating a supportive culture and, therefore, for developing a high-performing team. If you encounter anyone who thinks of inclusion as a 'buzzword' that has little value, I suggest you ask them the following questions.

Why would an organisation wish to have access to *less* than the full amount of human talent that could be at its disposal? Shouldn't organisations want to access the very best and brightest, who can leverage their expertise in service of organisational outcomes?

These are the questions high-performing teams will have considered and built an inclusive culture around.

High-performing teams create inclusive cultures where every team member feels valued, respected and empowered to bring their authentic selves to work. They recognise the importance of diversity, equity, belonging and inclusion in driving innovation, fostering creativity and enhancing organisational performance. Inclusive businesses tend to have more equitable policies and practices regarding pay and opportunities for advancement.

If a business doesn't have an inclusive culture, the company's employees may predominantly come from similar backgrounds. By some measure or another, there will be a lack of diversity be that in terms of race, gender, ethnicity, age or another demographic factor. Without inclusivity, a team that is made up of individuals from diverse backgrounds will not achieve its full potential. Research from Korn Ferry found that inclusive teams make better decisions 87% of the time, compared to their less-inclusive counterparts.[1]

It is important to realise, though, that regardless of the make-up of a team, a lack of inclusive leadership will have a fundamental impact on decision-making and problem-solving as diverse perspectives are side-lined or ignored altogether. In this environment, it becomes harder to attract and retain talent and the team finds it harder to compete.

Consider how inclusive your team is. Do all employees feel valued and supported or that they belong at the organisation? Are there significant disparities in pay and opportunities for advancement among different groups of employees?

Examples of Inclusion

Determining the 'most inclusive' businesses can be subjective and depends on various factors such as diversity initiatives, policies, workplace culture and employee feedback. Diversity also means different things in different cultures. In North America, there is a greater focus on ethnicity, in Europe on gender and sexual orientation and in Asia on socioeconomic background.

As I write this in 2025, Diversity, Equity and Inclusion (DEI) has become a political hot potato in the United States, with some organisations publicly abandoning DEI initiatives, while others reframe them using terms such as 'workplace culture' or 'belonging'. This is why focusing on inclusion is crucial—everyone needs to feel included to perform at their best. Inclusion is not about pitting one group against another, or saying that one demographic is more important than another, but about everyone feeling comfortable to bring their differing life experiences and skills to the table to contribute more as a team.

Often, however, inclusion goes hand in hand with diversity, and several companies have gained recognition for their efforts in fostering inclusivity and diversity within their organisations.

Unilever, for example, has set ambitious goals to promote a more equitable and inclusive society. Key commitments include ensuring that all workers providing goods and services to the company earn a living wage by 2030 and investing €2 billion annually in suppliers from underrepresented groups by 2025. This investment is part of its drive to eliminate biases in recruitment. Meanwhile, Unilever supports vulnerable workers in sectors like manufacturing and agriculture by collaborating with suppliers, NGOs and governments to promote living wage practices. The company also aims to equip 10 million young people with essential job skills by 2030.

The evolving nature of work, both during and post-COVID, also led to a commitment to ensure that all employees were reskilled or upskilled by 2025. Through partnerships and initiatives like the LevelUp platform, Unilever committed to preparing the next generation for future job opportunities, ultimately linking social equity to business success.

For Unilever, inclusion also means responsible advertising. In 2004, it launched its 'Campaign for Real Beauty' via its Dove brand. Discarding stereotypes, the brand broke with convention by featuring real women instead of models in its ads—a move that resonated with audiences all over the world. In 2023, Dove delivered €6 billion in turnover for Unilever, and the 'Dove Self-Esteem Project' reached over 100 million young lives with body confidence education.

In the realm of B2B, Salesforce is widely recognised for its 'Ohana' culture, which embodies the principles of trust, equality and a sense of belonging. The term 'Ohana', meaning family in Hawaiian, reflects Salesforce's commitment to creating a supportive environment where every employee feels valued and included. This culture is foundational to the company's operations and is integral to its business strategy.

To promote diversity and inclusion, Salesforce has implemented several initiatives aimed at fostering a more equitable workplace. The company focuses on equal pay, conducting regular audits to ensure that employees receive fair compensation regardless of gender, race, or other factors. This commitment to pay equity is a critical component of Salesforce's strategy to address systemic inequalities within the tech industry.

Salesforce also emphasises diverse hiring practices, aiming to build a workforce that reflects the communities it serves. The company actively recruits candidates from underrepresented groups and provides training programs to ensure a smooth transition into the workplace. Employee resource groups (ERGs) play a significant role in this effort, offering support and networking opportunities for employees who share common backgrounds or experiences. These groups foster a sense of community and enable employees to engage with one another on various issues, from career development to social justice.

Allyship training also equips Salesforce employees with the tools they need to support their colleagues actively. This training encourages individuals to become advocates for their peers, creating a culture of mutual respect and understanding.

Similar to Unilever, Salesforce has also invested beyond its internal efforts, prioritising social responsibility and philanthropy. The company engages in numerous initiatives designed to address societal challenges, including education, equality and environmental sustainability. Salesforce's 1-1-1 model—committing 1% of equity, 1% of employee time and 1% of product to philanthropic efforts—underscores its dedication to creating positive social change.

By fostering a culture of Ohana and prioritising diversity, inclusion and social responsibility, Salesforce not only enhances its workplace environment but also contributes to a more equitable society. This holistic approach to corporate responsibility has positioned Salesforce as a leader in the tech industry and serves as a model for other organisations striving to create inclusive work cultures.

Creating an inclusive work culture means giving everyone a chance to share their perspectives and ensuring that everyone has access to the same opportunities. Psychological safety and resilience play into this. As a team, what steps do you take to make sure everyone feels included? How do you integrate new team members when they join? Can you identify any barriers to inclusion in your workplace and what could you do to address these?

In Conversation with Alim Dhanji, Chief HR Officer TD SYNNEX

In a career spanning over 25 years, Alim has seen the landscape around DEI evolve in many different ways. With his personal experiences as an LGBT person of colour, as well as his extensive professional experience in many large organisations, Alim was the ideal person to speak to about inclusion and he shared some fascinating insights on the topic.

MARC: *How important is inclusion in terms of a cultural attribute for any organisation that you're part of?*

ALIM: I think any company that strives to be high performance, and certainly we do at TD SYNNEX, needs to have psychological safety as an attribute and people have got to be able to be authentically themselves. That means they've got to be empowered without fear of retaliation. They've got to be able to speak up and feel that their voice will be heard. Those are all contributors to psychological safety. When you have psychological safety, we're really talking about having an environment that's inclusive.

Inclusion, as an element of DEI, is being scrutinised for strange reasons because of the politics that have been going on, but I can't see any business thriving without having a commitment to inclusion.

It affects not only your ability to attract and retain the very best, but also their ability to be optimal and high performing.

I have seen this first hand as President at a leading Fortune 100 brand, accountable for significant commercial success. If you don't have inclusive teams, and you don't have an inclusive perspective, it can affect your ability to be competitive in the market. I, therefore, feel inclusion is both an employee attraction, retention, and engagement imperative, and a market advantage.

MARC: *What's the thing within the current business that you're most proud of?*

ALIM: When I joined the company, like many other companies that espouse their values, TD SYNNEX was talking about servant leadership. I wasn't sure if this was just textbook talk, because it's very hard to implement servant leadership as you need consistency and low ego across your leadership levels. Although TD SYNNEX is a smaller organisation relative to where I've been before, it still employs 24,000 people. So, before I started in my role, I was wondering how they implemented servant leadership, especially because we operate in 55 countries. But when I joined it was evident to me that it is not just a program here. We are hearing a lot about rollbacks on DEI policies, but there's nothing to roll back here. At TD SYNNEX, it is sincerely part of the mutual respect that we have for each other and the genuine care that we have for each other. It's embedded into the ethos of servant leadership that we are first and foremost responsible for removing the roadblocks to create environments for success. Therefore, if one of those roadblocks is an inability to be yourself, feeling disempowered to speak up or not feeling included, then we're not doing our jobs as leaders.

Servant leadership, and by association inclusion, is central to its very core to how we are supposed to show up as leaders, how we get developed as leaders and how we are held accountable and compensated as leaders. It's really ingrained and embedded.

MARC: *If you want to create a more inclusive environment, it's challenging now, especially in the United States, because of the politics around just the word itself. What advice would you have for those who are trying to do that whilst navigating these external pressures?*

ALIM: My lesson has been learned the hard way at other businesses. Sometimes, as well as a genuine desire to show that an organisation is sincere in wanting to change things, the response to a crisis is somewhat motivated by PR. Create some shock and awe.

A business might say, 'We're giving $100 million every year to BIPOC (Black, Indigenous, and People of Colour) communities. We're going to have X percent of our leaders by this year who are BIPOC or women'. All these grand commitments are made. But three years later, many organisations have realised that they've overcommitted and now they see a window with politics, particularly in the United States, to get out. Some may be using the change in political climate as a way to bow out. They were never going to achieve those targets. But now they can say, 'Well, the world has changed, and so we've changed our targets'.

MARC: *Is it easier to distinguish between inclusion with a capital I, the DEI-type inclusion, and being generally inclusive in the way you operate day to day? Is that a starting point?*

ALIM: Definitely, because by definition, you're not getting into targets that exclude. Take Employee Resource Groups (ESGs), which are so powerful, as an example. They're culture carriers, and they've been around for many years. But all of a sudden they're getting heat, because if you're part of an ERG, you're excluding others. That was never the intent. It was never the intent to have an LGBT ERG that excludes people who are not LGBT. In fact, you want more people who are not to be part of an LGBT ERG, because then it shows the commitment and the allyship within your organisation. But somehow ERGs have become fashioned as groups that meet after hours to collude and create a force to reckon, and even unionise, when that's not the intent.

I think inclusion is the fundamental part of DEI, so you have to start there. You want to be able to speak to everybody, regardless of race, socioeconomic background or anything else. I was talking the other day with someone who has been teaching me a lot about menopause. It sounds odd to say that as a male, but the disadvantages that women of a certain age in an organisation experience when they're going through menopause are significant, and their career gets limited because we are not recognising that they're going through something that we need to support them with. Learning about those experiences is a form of inclusion.

You're never going to have an ERG for menopause, but fundamentally, what you want are leaders who are thoughtful, have the right conversations and create the right environments, and also have policies that underwrite support for everybody and not just certain groups. That's what creates that foundation for inclusion. That's a good starting point.

MARC: *And from your experience as an HR leader, what are the things that you spot when things aren't as inclusive as they should be?*

ALIM: I've been in companies where, in some forums, certain people would not speak up. And it was very visible. That gave me an indication right away that it's not an environment where, if you don't hold a certain grade level, or you're not part of a certain academic background, you don't have the invitation to speak. The message that comes across is, 'You can listen, but you're not as valued'. So I think one sign is, are you invited? Do people speak up freely? If you don't see that happening, then it's not necessarily an inclusive environment.

Number two is when you track exit interviews and measure employees' sentiment throughout the year. I think that's a very data-rich way to understand whether you're inclusive or not. Third, if the right policies don't exist in the organisation around, say, anti-racism or anti-retaliation, there's no safety net. If you don't have that safety net, people feel much more vulnerable. Let's face it, the older you get and the more responsibilities you have—like a mortgage, a car and kids—the less risk you take. That's just natural. So as you get through that phase in life, you're going to take less risk and feel less secure to speak up if you don't have certain policies that protect you in an organisation.

MARC: *It's interesting you use the word risk there. One of the excuses people make around inclusion is that they would rather say nothing than say something and get it wrong.*

ALIM: I think cancel culture has a lot to do with this, and what's happened over the last few years is whether it's a town hall or just a simple team meeting, leaders have had to review their script over and over again because they're scared to say the wrong thing. When I talk about psychological safety, it's not meant to be just for junior employees. That psychological safety needs to be extended to leaders as well. Otherwise, you're just pushing each other away rather than coming together to undo the knot. When people feel scared of saying the wrong thing, it's as though everyone ends up pulling the thread into knots, which become tighter and tighter; and more and more difficult to untangle.

Very effective leaders who I admired were declining to go on stage because they were scared of saying the wrong thing. This was, in part, because they saw what happened to me at a previous business. I'm obviously a person of colour, I'm LGBT and I was talking to a group of people about how I came out and my experience within the business. It was all done with good intent, but it was flipped, and put on Instagram, where it was positioned as 'easy for me to say', because I've got the privilege of my status in the organisation, and my career level.

That was actually good for me to go through, because I understood what other leaders were facing. I thought I was spared. I was not. So then I started talking more with employees and explaining that if we want leaders to engage, we can't be throwing rocks at our own house. We've really got to come together to talk. I think that things are starting to change, but it's so charged right now because the pendulum has swung from woke to anti-woke, and it's a battle.

For example, at a previous organisation, I posted on LinkedIn about our business achieving a perfect score on the Corporate Equality Index, but there was a discussion internally about whether we should post at all. This is what paralyses organisations. This recognition is something to be proud of. It's a difficult thing to get, so why wouldn't we be proud of that? But many organisations are pausing because they're concerned about the backlash. Perhaps this is a more acute issue for larger, consumer facing brands. I know my peers at Apple and Meta and others are in a different position altogether because the scrutiny is very strong. What I come back to is what's our mission? What's our purpose? What are our values? And how do we then lean into them to inform our decisions about DEI? We come back to the same thing: for us, our behaviour has never been target-led or a program, it is just inclusion.

MARC: *How can leaders foster more inclusive environments on a day-to-day basis? What are the behaviours you want to see?*

ALIM: One thing I learned only a few years ago is not to start with assumptions of what the workforce needs and that there's tremendous power in listening. I once undertook 200 listening sessions across an organisation, and I wish we had done that before we had committed to a variety of different targets, because the targets we set were not what our employees wanted. What they wanted was to be seen and heard. They wanted to know that their experience was understood. One individual I spoke with in LA, shared with me that when he wakes up in the morning he has to go on an app to understand where the police checks are so that he doesn't get stopped on his way to work. The guy has a PhD from Berkeley, but he happens to be black, and so every day he has to think about that. It brought tears to my eyes that he had to go through that every day just to get to work.

I was hearing stories from women, from people who are close to retirement who have a perception they have no value, to people who have dyslexia or are from single-parent families. If you just listen, it helps to inform what basic policies and support mechanisms you need to have in the organisation. It's not about committing millions of dollars. They don't want these grand gestures. That's a PR stunt. Listening is so powerful. When you listen, you better your understanding of what the themes are, what actions to prioritise and then you can take action and communicate about those actions to the rest of the organisation. It's nothing profound but requires patience and a genuine desire to understand others' lived experiences.

One thing that I've done at this organisation is increased the mandate for the VP responsible for DEI so it includes employee listening. This involves aggregating all the different touch points—the employee survey, the onboarding interviews, exit interviews, and we also collect rich data from employee relations cases and round tables, as well as town halls. This gives us a list of all the questions that surface every month. She is tasked to give us a more well-rounded point of view about what our co-workers feel on an ongoing basis, and that's the feedback loop that informs our leadership behaviours, our HR programs and what we might communicate in our town halls.

MARC: *Is there anything else that you want to share about high performance?*

ALIM: I've been doing a lot of reading about high performance, and the thing that stands out to me over and over again is accountability. If you have leaders who don't have clear goals that align towards the organisation and then cascade, it creates a break in accountability. I've seen so many organisations that don't get it right, so it's good to see goal setting and accountability in your model.

I really appreciated Alim's openness and honesty in our discussion. Here are my top three takeaways from our talk:

1. *Psychological safety and inclusion go hand in hand. You can't have one without the other and it's a leader's role to ensure that everyone on their team feels able to speak up and be heard.*

2. *Leaders also need to feel psychologically safe, especially in an era that is becoming defined by 'cancel culture'.*

3. *One of the most powerful things any leader can do to create a more inclusive environment is listen. Not only does this lead to more impactful changes in an organisational culture, it is often also a lot more cost-effective than introducing headline-grabbing initiatives.*

Both Alim and Andria talked about the need for the individuals within their teams to bond and the importance of creating a sense of belonging for everyone who works at an organisation. When everyone on a team feels they belong, it indicates that you have created an inclusive environment, where each person feels free to be themselves, which in turn allows them to do their best work. Without that sense of belonging, you will struggle to achieve high performance.

Leaders as Coach

Creating a sense of belonging directly addresses the emotional and psychological needs that foster inclusive behaviours and environments. When people feel they belong, they are confident that they can express themselves without fear of judgment or exclusion. This encourages individuals to share their ideas, voice concerns and contribute their unique perspectives. This is particularly true for those from underrepresented or marginalised groups.

(continued)

(continued)

Individuals who feel unseen or excluded can become disengaged, but a strong sense of belonging affirms that every team member is valued and accepted for who they are, regardless of their background, identity or differences.

When individuals feel included and valued, they are more likely to bring their authentic selves to work and share their unique ideas and experiences. This diversity of thought enriches the team's creativity and problem-solving abilities, driving innovation and better decision-making.

In essence, belonging is the emotional foundation of inclusion. While inclusion focuses on actions to involve and respect diverse individuals, belonging ensures that these efforts resonate personally, making people feel genuinely valued and connected. Together, they create stronger, more innovative and more equitable teams.

Process

The exercise I like to use to start building a sense of belonging whilst simultaneously celebrating the differences amongst others is 'The Story Behind Our Names'.

Objective: Enhance a sense of belonging and trust within the team by sharing personal stories related to names and providing insight into each team member's background, values and heritage.

Purpose: Explain that the goal of the activity is to strengthen team connections by learning about the unique stories and meanings behind each person's name.

Guidelines: Encourage openness, curiosity and respect for everyone's story. Emphasise that this is a safe space to share personal experiences.

Sharing stories: Invite each team member to share their full name and the story behind it, covering topics such as:

- Who chose their name and the reason behind it?

- Any funny, interesting or meaningful stories associated with their name.

- How do they feel about their name and do they go by a nickname or another name?

For example: 'My name is Marc Patrick Woods. I was born in the United Kingdom, where Mark is traditionally spelt with a K, but my parents thought spelling it with a C was exotic. My middle name, Patrick, comes from my father. And my surname probably reflects that someone in my ancestry lived near the woods. At school, I was nicknamed 'Woody Woodpecker' after the cartoon character'.

Encourage others to ask follow-up questions to show interest and learn more.

- What does your name mean in your culture?

- How has your name shaped your experiences?

Reflection and group discussion: After everyone has shared, facilitate a group discussion using prompts like:

- What stories or details surprised you about your teammates?

- How did it feel to share something personal about your name?

- How can knowing these stories strengthen our connection as a team?

(continued)

(continued)

> **Wrap-up**: Conclude by highlighting the unique diversity of the team and how each person's background and identity contribute to the team's collective strength.
>
> ## Why It Works
>
> Sharing personal stories fosters vulnerability, and learning about each other's backgrounds helps team members understand and appreciate each other's perspectives.
>
> This simple yet impactful activity reminds team members that their individuality contributes to the team's collective strength.

14

How a One Team Ethos Maintains High Performance

When you bring not only resilience, psychological safety and inclusion together, but also the other eight attributes in my Best Teams Model, you will have a team of individuals who excel when they work together. But as Andria pointed out, the makeup of a team can change. How can you ensure that your team consistently performs to the best of its ability, even in the face of change? The answer is by developing a One Team Ethos.

I have been privileged to be part of several fabulous teams, but for me there was one which stands out. I knew it was high-performing not because of the gold medal it won in Athens, or the obvious camaraderie between the swimmers. Rather, it was when the person who was responsible for keeping the water clean in my pool came up to me and said how much he had enjoyed watching the Athens Paralympics on television and how proud he was to see the team doing so well. Then, he said something that made all the focus on being a high-performing team worthwhile: 'I am part of that team, aren't I?' And he was.

In that moment, he displayed our One Team Ethos—a belief that everyone had a role to play.

If a business has a One Team Ethos, employees from different departments or levels of hierarchy work together seamlessly toward common goals, fostering a sense of unity and camaraderie. Teams collaborate across functional areas to solve problems, innovate and deliver high-quality products or services. Employees are willing to step outside of their traditional roles or job descriptions to support team members or address emerging needs within the organisation.

If a business doesn't have a One Team Ethos, teams may operate in isolation, with little communication or collaboration between them, leading to duplication of efforts and inefficiencies. Employees prioritise individual or departmental goals over the collective success of the organisation, leading to rivalry, resentment and a lack of cooperation. When problems arise, individuals or departments may engage in finger-pointing and scapegoating rather than working together to address issues constructively.

To have a One Team Ethos, there must be transparency and open dialogue, with information openly shared across teams or departments, enabling effective decision-making and problem-solving.

Consider your team. Does each individual understand their role in the overall success of the team? Do they have a sense of belonging and feel valued? Do they support each other regardless of hierarchy or job description? If not, then they don't have a One Team Ethos.

There's No 'I' in 'Team'

Legend has it that President John F. Kennedy was taking a tour of NASA, stopping occasionally to talk to the employees. 'What's your job at the facility?' the President asked one man. 'My job is to help put a man on the Moon', the man replied. He was a janitor.

It's a great illustration of the power and scope of teams. No person could put a man on the Moon on their own, yet in a specialised team they managed it. And the janitor? He was as much a part of the team as the top scientists or the astronauts. If he had performed the tasks assigned to him badly, he could have prevented one of the greatest achievements of the human race.

A One Team Ethos is essential for fostering resilience, innovation and success within organisations. This ethos encourages unity and shared purpose, bridging departments and enabling employees to work together to achieve common goals. By cultivating a collaborative environment rooted in trust, empathy and shared values, companies create a foundation for sustainable growth, regardless of the challenges they encounter. Examples from companies like HubSpot, Atlassian, Zappos and Southwest Airlines illustrate how a strong, one-team culture drives collective success and a supportive workplace.

Building a Collaborative 'Culture Code'

HubSpot is widely known for its 'Culture Code'—a set of guiding principles emphasising teamwork, transparency and empathy. HubSpot's ethos prioritises collaboration across departments, where employees work together to reach shared goals and embrace diverse perspectives. HubSpot also values diversity, inclusion and authenticity, helping employees feel respected and supported as part of one unified team.

This collaborative environment is bolstered by HubSpot's commitment to transparency; employees have access to open communication channels, including meetings and platforms that promote shared insights and collective progress. In HubSpot's environment, employees thrive on a foundation of trust and respect, which enhances their ability to innovate and work toward company objectives.

Fostering Unity Through the 'Team Playbook'

Atlassian promotes a strong one-team culture with its 'Team Playbook' initiative. This framework encourages teamwork, transparency and continuous improvement as central pillars of the workplace experience. By prioritising collaboration across teams, employees are encouraged to leverage their diverse skills and perspectives to tackle complex challenges.

Psychological safety is a cornerstone of this ethos, as employees are encouraged to take calculated risks, voice opinions and learn from both successes and mistakes. The 'Team Playbook' serves as a guide, providing employees with tools and resources to work cohesively and address problems as a unified front. Atlassian's dedication to this framework has helped the company create an agile, responsive culture capable of adapting to evolving industry demands.

A 'Zapponian' Culture of Empowerment and Unity

Zappos, known for its unique corporate culture, embodies the One Team Ethos through its 'Zapponian' culture, where collaboration, transparency and a sense of belonging are key priorities. Zappos takes a distinct approach with its 'holacratic' organisational structure, which promotes self-management and cross-functional collaboration. Employees are empowered to work together without traditional hierarchies, fostering an environment of equality and mutual respect.

This structure encourages Zappos employees to innovate, solve problems and work together to create exceptional customer experiences. Additionally, Zappos values open communication and teamwork across all levels, promoting a culture where every employee feels empowered to contribute to the company's goals. By fostering an atmosphere of mutual support and collaboration, Zappos enhances both employee satisfaction and customer service, reinforcing a strong sense of unity within the organisation.

Nurturing a 'Warrior Spirit'

Southwest Airlines has cultivated a reputation for its 'Warrior Spirit'—a philosophy that centres around teamwork, shared responsibility and a family-like culture. Employees across Southwest Airlines are encouraged to work together to uphold the company's values, delivering excellent customer service and contributing to a supportive workplace.

Southwest fosters camaraderie and mutual respect, promoting a culture where employees feel like they are part of a larger family. By encouraging employees to work together and contribute to shared objectives, Southwest has built a team-centric atmosphere where everyone feels responsible for the success of the company. This approach has led to Southwest's strong brand identity and customer loyalty, as employees' shared commitment to the company's mission reflects positively on customer interactions and company growth.

The Impact of a Unified Team Culture

These companies demonstrate the power of a One Team Ethos to build resilience and drive success. A unified team culture enables companies to adapt to challenges, foster creativity and align employees with a common mission. By prioritising collaboration, transparency and inclusivity, these organisations empower their teams to achieve collective success. HubSpot's 'Culture Code', Atlassian's 'Team Playbook', Zappos' 'holacratic' structure and Southwest's 'Warrior Spirit' offer models for other organisations aiming to cultivate unity and a shared sense of purpose.

One of the elements that stand out in all of these examples is the effort they have taken to create unity not only within individual teams, but across entire organisations. When you look at your team, do you feel as though everyone on it is pulling in the same direction? If not, which attributes that we've covered so far could help you achieve this unity? Do you need a strong shared goal or purpose? Perhaps clearer communication would help? Or do you need to work on creating an open culture where everyone feels safe to share and learn from their mistakes? Often the missing ingredient in a One Team Ethos will be one of the attributes I've already covered.

In Conversation with Pedro De La Rosa, Aston Martin F1 Team Ambassador

As a former F1 driver and now an Aston Martin Aramco Formula One™ Team Ambassador, Pedro de la Rosa knows what it takes to be part of a high-performing team. Formula One is often held up as a shining example of a One Team Ethos, but as Pedro explained, there's a lot more to embodying this ethos than a slick pit stop—and not every team gets it right.

Marc: *In an F1 team, everybody focuses on the driver. Can you explain a little about all the different layers of the team behind the driver?*

Pedro: When I started in Formula One, being a reserve driver involved a lot of testing. Now you have a very limited number of days during the year that you can really test, but you still have the test team and the simulator team learning how to best set up the car and helping the team with a development program. Being a reserve driver involves a lot of waiting. You can spend years waiting for your chance, so you need to feel part of the team to deal with that.

Marc: *Then you've also got the marketing and commercial teams; Aston Martin Aramco employs over 1,000 people. How important is it that they have the same kind of focus and belief?*

Pedro: You have to feel part of it, even if you're not trackside. The race team obviously have the most adrenaline-fuelled job; they face the enemy every weekend. They have the privilege to deliver on site. But if they fail, they are letting 1,000 families down—that's a great pressure. But feeling that pressure means that your work is very relevant, and everyone in the world can see if you're doing a good or a bad job.

The important thing for any of those trackside people is to carry over that adrenaline into the factory and help those working behind the scenes to understand that the result will also depend on their day-to-day job. You cannot compete if you don't have the tools to fight against your competitors. The key is to make sure everyone in the race team translates that amount of pressure, that feeling, to those working elsewhere in the organisation. In doing so, you get the support to be able to win races.

The reserve driver plays an important role in this, because they are not only trackside, but also spend a lot of time in the simulator at the factory. If you have the wrong attitude in this role, it can be detrimental for the whole team. If you don't believe what you're doing is important, that feeling can permeate through to others.

I always had the belief that this weekend could be my weekend. I was a particularly good reserve driver, but it had nothing to do with my speed or my feedback; it was down to my attitude. I would not let the team down, and they could see this. I thought that was normal, but now I look at other reserve drivers and realise they may be the fastest, the most complete, or the most skilful, but if they don't have the right attitude, I would never have them on my team because it's contagious. You can be positively contagious or negatively contagious.

At the end of the day, we have to make sure that the 1,000 people who work here feel part of the organisation and that they're accountable for performance.

Whatever your role, you have to bring the right attitude to the factory.

Marc: *How do you encourage the right attitude when you are at the factory?*

Pedro: In my role as Team Ambassador, I don't have any direct influence on performance or reliability, but I do feel part of it. When the team is on the podium, I feel very proud. Everyone in a team needs that feeling, because when you create the right environment in Formula One, you win, but without making every member of the team feel important, you will never win.

I never doubt that our guys are the most talented in the business, but that's not enough. You also have to create the best environment for these people. How can you do that? This is the million dollar question. The first step is to make sure that when you say 'we are a family', or 'we have a culture', you really have a culture, and you really feel like a family, because when your family members have problems, you need to support them.

I went into a team once in the past and the first thing they said to me when I arrived was, 'Welcome to the family', which was encouraging. But in that same meeting, they said to me, 'Pedro, remember one thing, this brand is bigger than the people and the drivers. We are more than a team'. When they said that, I realised it was the wrong culture and that when things went wrong and the pressure built up, they would start firing people like there was no tomorrow. For me, this is the wrong attitude to start a relationship with.

Marc: *What is the right attitude?*

Pedro: To always spend as much time with your people as you can. Everyone in the race team has to show an interest in what other people are providing them with at the race track. It's important to show genuine interest in the people, what they do and to make sure that they feel that their work makes a difference.

I really love what people do. I'm not doing work that is related to performance anymore, but I'm still very interested in how we can achieve performance and how we can all be better. When I do a marketing or commercial event, or when I speak on Spanish TV, I want to know what I'm talking about and who does what. That's what makes me feel like I'm truly part of a family.

The most important attribute of any team member is to feel that what you are doing is special no matter what you're doing. Because I am. Whenever I do a marketing event, I always say to myself, 'Do it 100%. Just do it as well as you can, as if it was a test day or a race day'. You need to give it your all, and that's how I expect everyone to behave in the factory as well.

Marc: *Everyone knows a little about the pit stop but can you explain how the pit stop team comes together?*

Pedro: There are 24 mechanics in the garage who all participate somehow in a pit stop. We need around 17 people for the pit stop itself, but there are others that come into play, for example, if there is an accident and there's a nose change in the pit stop. You need to cover all scenarios. All of these mechanics really all want to be part of it and it's very competitive just to be there. If the mechanic doesn't feel right or they have lost a bit of confidence in the last race, you rotate them and pick the strongest person at that point. They have to have a positive attitude and are competitive by nature; they really push each other.

We have a pit stop simulator, and they have special training programs—because the rear tyre weighs 23 kilos and the front tyre is 20 kilos. We film all the pit stops to see if they can improve any movement or coordination between them. There is also a psychologist to help them. All to make sure that they are in perfect physical and psychological shape.

It's just an amazing team effort. But the most encouraging thing for me is the fact that when a mechanic is not in the pit stop, they are not happy. They are very competitive.

There was once a proposal to get all the mechanics wearing overalls with a number and their names, but the teams decided against it because it was adding too much pressure. Between them, they know who is who, but I think for the outside world, it's better not to be named if you make a mistake. Because in a pit stop, you are remembered for the mistakes. Everyone is expecting a two second pit stop. If you are over 2.5 or three seconds, then the media always blames it on someone.

Marc: *You mention the public or media will look to blame somebody if they don't get it right. How do they deal with that within the team itself?*

Pedro: I think we go back to the culture again and how we support each other. At Aston Martin, we say it is perfectly normal to make mistakes, but it is unacceptable not to learn from them. Whenever anyone has made a mistake, we try to give them more confidence. If someone makes a mistake on a pit stop, we make sure that we don't change them for the next race unless they are not feeling like it. You try to recover by giving them extra confidence rather than stepping them down. You have to maintain a good state of mind for both the mechanics and the drivers. Saying it is easy; actually doing it under pressure is much more complicated.

Marc: *And of course there is competition within the team as there are two cars, two drivers, two crews at every race.*

Pedro: That's right. This is the nature of our sport. Your teammate is your biggest competitor, because he's the only one racing with the same equipment as yourself. On the other hand, you need to work as a team, because if you don't share information and you are not fully open, you won't be able to develop the car and you will not achieve the best results.

There are teams where there is big rivalry between race drivers, but they end up paying the price. You start dividing the garage in two, and when you divide a garage in two, it means that the information is not flowing from one side to the other as it should. You start generating division in the team between mechanics, engineers and even in the factory when they're producing a part and they know which driver it's for. That's very dangerous in this sport. So, it's the responsibility of the race drivers and the team principal to make sure that this culture is correct.

The team principal in particular needs to be able to sit down with key people in the team, to tell them what's wrong and what they want, and do it in a good way so that the relationships keep flowing.

Marc: *How many parts can be changed on the car, and how much of the car is different at the end of the season from the car which starts the season?*

Pedro: There are 13,000 parts and normally around 70% of the car has changed from the beginning of the year to the end of the year because the specifications for parts evolve. They change to contribute to a better performance. Sometimes that change makes the car more reliable, which is also very important. We focus on performance in Formula One, but there is also a big part of the team that concentrates on reliability or making the car safer. So, it is a balance between performance, reliability and safety.

Normally, a large amount of the car is new aerodynamically because aerodynamics are the biggest differentiator and the cheapest way of making the car faster. Therefore, the biggest part of the budget goes into aerodynamics, and that's a very important point. In the past, when I entered Formula One, engineers were always talking about making a car go faster. Nowadays, when you go to any meeting or listen to engineers, they mainly talk about how much money they can spend on making the car go faster. This is because we have a cost cap, and therefore a limited budget to spend on aerodynamics, on the mechanical side or on design. But one really interesting thing I see now is the collaboration between departments trying to get that money channelled to the most impactful place.

In the past, when you were designing the suspension, and you had X amount of money to invest in making the car faster, you would not give that away. But nowadays, if the aero department comes up with a new floor, but they have no money left to invest in that part, then they sit down with the mechanical engineers and discuss how they can use that money in the best possible way to make the car faster. What is more impactful? The cost cap has changed our mindset completely.

Marc: *How empowered are people? I'm thinking specifically if they see an opportunity to improve or avoid an issue.*

Pedro: The most successful Formula One teams are data driven. So if there is anything on the data that shows the tyres won't make it to the planned pit stop, they have to raise the flag. The thing is that some organisations say they are data driven, but when the engineer flags an issue in the middle of a race which is potentially going to put a podium finish in jeopardy, and the driver is screaming on the radio. 'These tyres are fine. I don't want to make a change'. Who do you listen to?

The reality is that the most successful teams are the ones that are purely data driven. You have to believe in your own data. We have over 200 sensors in the engine, 200 more in the chassis. We have 26 sensors on each of the tyres, checking the surface temperature, the pressure and the inner bulk temperature. We have people behind each channel of data analysing it; we have AI to tell us what is important and what is not. But if you don't listen to your people, to your engineers, and just try a brave manoeuvre because the driver feels that the tyres are okay, then you make more mistakes more often. At the end of the day, the team that makes the least mistakes in Formula One always wins.

Marc: *So, you have to trust your processes and trust your people?*

Pedro: Yes, you have to trust your processes, your data and especially your engineers. When they raise their hand, you have to trust them, and if they make a mistake, no problem, you don't suddenly change your culture overnight. Being consistent is the key. Then, make sure you give credit to all those people who are working for you. On the trackside, we have our 58 operational passes, plus two drivers. They are in the first line of fire. Then, we have almost 1,000 more in the factory and mission control, analysing all these data. We have strategies for the best possible combinations and strategies according to the life span of the tyre, or the engine. So, we are very dependent on our mission control team, and this is beautiful to watch because it means that we have the right culture.

Marc: *What piece of advice would you give to someone joining the Aston Martin Aramco Formula One team?*

Pedro: The thing that struck me most when I came into Aston Martin Aramco was how open they were. We still have this great mentality of being open.

For example, how the technical team works with the partners, the sponsors and the marketing team, and how much they share among themselves. When I was at other teams, they would say, 'Oh, we don't share this type of information with the marketing team', or 'Don't tell them this', or 'Just be very careful what you say to the press'.

Here, we are a lot more open, genuine and authentic, which makes people feel very safe in their work environment. If you control what people say and do, they lose all their creativity, and it becomes a very ugly environment.

So my advice: just be open. Because if you keep that type of openness, you will have a massive advantage over the rest.

I very much enjoyed my conversation with Pedro and it's interesting to hear his take on the One Team Ethos. These are my three top takeaways from our conversation:

1. *No matter what you do, do it to the best of your ability. The right attitude is contagious in a positive way, whereas the wrong attitude has negative consequences.*

2. *Ensure that everyone knows how their work contributes to overall performance and progress for the organisation.*

3. *Be open, share freely within the organisation and encourage creativity to get the best out of everyone.*

What struck me as I talked to Pedro was how many of the attributes of the Best Teams Model he mentioned in relation to having a One Team Ethos. He alluded to work ethic, autonomy, accountability, goal setting, psychological safety, integrity, communication, inclusivity, having a growth mindset, recognition and resilience. In fact, every single interview I've conducted for this book covers multiple attributes. The reason is simple—to create a high-performing team, there is no 'magic bullet'. The truth is that you need to bring together multiple elements to create a culture that is innovative, forward-thinking, collaborative and high-performing.

Leader as Coach

As you have read through these chapters, you will have noticed that many of the attributes of high-performing teams are interconnected, and this is particularly the case for creating a One Team Ethos. Many of the attributes need to be present for there to be a sense that we are all in this together.

I regularly get asked to support teams of people with a strong work ethic who communicate well and are respectful and inclusive. 'Can you help us create a One Team Ethos?' is often their main question.

There are numerous ways to do this, and below is a process I have found particularly fruitful in bringing people together and providing an output they can refer back to. To do this thoroughly will take approximately half a day, but if you feel the team would benefit from some time considering psychological safety, then I would make it a full day offsite.

(continued)

(continued)

Process

Step 1

Ask the people attending to complete a 'User Manual' as pre-work. If I were attending as a participant, I would therefore be creating a 'User Manual to working with Marc'. The following are examples of questions you could use:

Individual level

○ I do my best work when. . .

○ My three biggest strengths are. . .

○ My two key development areas are. . .

○ My main motivator at work is. . .

○ Something that really irritates me at work is. . .

○ When I am under pressure, I like to work in the following way. . .

○ My confidence dips when. . .

○ To relax and recharge, I like to. . .

Team level

○ What I will bring to the team. . .

○ How I like information to be communicated. . .

○ The best way to give me difficult/negative feedback is. . .

○ When challenging others, my style is more (choose one)

- *Direct & Disruptive*

- *Supportive & Collaborative*

○ When it comes to execution, my style is more (choose one)

- *Reflective & Strategic*

- *Pacey & Action Oriented*

Each participant then attends the offsite with their 'User Manual' to hand, either printed or electronically.

Step 2

Ask the participants to pair up and share their 'User Manual' with each other. Ideally, they would pair with someone they know less well or who they don't work with as frequently.

Step 3

Bring the group back together and ask each person to share what they learned about each other. Ask the group if they think they missed anything based on their experience of the individual. Capture all of the preferences and comments generated on a whiteboard, flip chart or electronically. However, you choose to do it, make sure everyone can see what is being written down.

Step 4

When everyone has shared, take a look at what has been captured and discuss two things. First, discuss the differences and acknowledge that differences are good for the team. Then, take a look at the similarities. If you are experienced in facilitating meetings like this, you will have been able to group the 'User Manual' preferences as they were being shared, but if you haven't, get the group to help you. Find five or so that everyone can agree are important to them. These then become the 'We will. . .' statements the group commits to. For example, they might be:

(continued)

(continued)

We will:

- **Prioritise trust and collaboration:** We will be authentic and partner with each other rather than working as individuals.

- **Communicate with *Radical Candor*:** We will have clear, direct and respectful communication across our organisation to create clarity, remove ambiguity and enable one another.

- **Execute with purpose:** We will move with pace as we hold ourselves accountable, staying focused on impactful actions to achieve our growth goals.

- **Deliver as ONE TEAM:** We will ensure our actions are aligned with the broader business strategy. . .*We Only Win If We All Win.*

- **Enjoy the journey:** We will embrace the opportunity ahead while celebrating the people we work with and the accomplishments we achieve together.

Step 5

Agree among the group that this will be the 'Team Charter' and encourage them to call each other out if one of these isn't being adhered to. Perhaps have it as the final slide for every team meeting so you can course correct in the moment.

Why It Works

I find this approach particularly impactful as it provides an opportunity for individuals to get to know each other better, celebrate their differences and coalesce around a shared set of values.

A Supportive Culture Underpins Success

Every organisation, large or small, has its own culture. However, a culture that nurtures and creates high-performing teams blends resilience, psychological safety and inclusion in such a way that they develop a One Team Ethos. This is what delivers true high performance at every level.

Arguably, the attributes that fall under the supportive culture element of my Best Teams Model are the most important because they underpin everything else I've covered in this book. As I mentioned earlier, often when you get the supportive culture aspect of the model right, many of the other elements naturally fall into place.

A supportive culture is like a living, breathing ecosystem, and it needs to be nurtured at every level. As a leader, this is one of the most important aspects of your role. When you can help everyone develop their resilience, make people feel safe and included and give people space and time to share their perspectives, you will create a team that not only supports one another, but also the wider organisation to achieve its goals.

15

The Ecosystem of High-Performing Teams

'It's the commitment to doing the difficult things daily that sets high-performing teams apart from the rest'. Matt Parker, Director of Innovation at the UK Institute of Sport, said this during our conversation, which you can read in full a little later in this chapter, and it really struck a chord with me.

Becoming a high-performing team, and then maintaining that level of performance, isn't easy. It is difficult. Throughout this book and my Best Teams Model, I've introduced you to 12 crucial attributes that are required. But what has stood out the most throughout my work, and the conversations I've had with organisational leaders for this book, is the interconnected nature of those attributes. You need to view them as essential components of a high-performance ecosystem, not as stand-alone boxes to be ticked.

Some of the attributes are more obviously related than others—such as goal setting and accountability; or inclusion and psychological safety—but they all support each other in one way or another. As leaders, our role is to ensure that each of the attributes is present in our teams and to find ways of nurturing any that are not as strong as the others.

In Conversation with Matt Parker, Director of Innovation at The UK Institute of Sport

I first met Matt in 2004, when he was my physiologist. Since that time, he's worked in multiple positions within high-performance sport, including as the Director of Marginal Gains at British Cycling under David Brailsford. Having worked alongside so many high-performing teams, he was the ideal person to speak to about how leaders, organisations and individuals can bring each of the attributes in the Best Teams Model together to deliver sustained high performance.

MARC: *When I think of how you and I first met, working with Lars Humer (Head Coach of the British Paralympic Swimming Team), it was clear you always tried to get the best out of people. What did you take from that period into your role at British Cycling?*

MATT: I often reflect on how fortunate I was to start my early journey in high-performance sport by working with Lars. The reason I took so much from that relationship is that we both shared a great curiosity for performance and we were just as fascinated by what we didn't know, as by what we did. That curiosity has stayed with me in everything

I do. I encourage everyone to question what they don't know about what we're doing, and it's often in that long list of unknowns that we uncover exciting opportunities we can explore.

Most of us are biased towards what we know and we take confidence from 'knowing'. But there is huge value in questioning what we believe to be true and having conversations about what we don't know. For some people, a list of unknowns creates anxiety and reduces confidence, but I find the opposite. When we start to shine a light on the areas that will give us a performance advantage if we can improve them more quickly than others, I find it increases both my confidence as a leader and that of my team.

When you get everyone in a room and ask them to talk about what they don't know, it can be awkward to start with. But in my experience, by the end of an hour, we'll have a wall full of Post-It notes of things we individually or collectively 'don't know' and we'll have built a relationship based on honesty and trust. I remember once questioning Lars about a training set he'd written on the poolside whiteboard for a future session just before the swimmers came in for their session. I asked him why he'd made particular choices about rest times, intensity and so on.

Throughout that training session, I'd see Lars looking over at the whiteboard, and when the swimmers had gone back to the locker room, he turned to me and said, 'I've looked at that in a number of different ways, and I think I'm right'.

I replied with, 'I think you're right too'. That was the moment I think we both realised that the real value in our relationship would come from that shared questioning and ensuring we'd explored what we didn't know as well as what we did.

I have never felt like an expert in anything, but over the years I've always tried to ask the right questions, at the right time, for the right people, with the right level of honesty.

MARC: *That's brilliant Matt. What needs to be in place for those conversations to be able to happen, or what challenges can stop those conversations from happening?*

MATT: I think you need a level of personal and professional credibility with the person you're speaking to. I deliberately say 'person' because I think you need to be mindful of the individual relationships you have with each person within a team, to view them appropriately as individual relationships, and to take the time to understand where you sit in those relationships. I'm talking about reflecting on what that person means to you, what you mean to them and what it means when you're together and collectively in a group.

I also believe it's hugely important to make the time to maintain your own personal understanding of that, and to check your assumptions around relationships regularly, because things change over time and with context.

Using my relationship with Lars as an example, I didn't turn up to work with him as an expert, but I had some expertise. My personal credibility in that relationship came from showing an interest in what he did and how he did it, rather than by believing I knew what I was doing. I added value by acknowledging what I didn't know, and asking those questions.

MARC: *What I've taken from this is that you have a growth mindset and integrity in terms of how you behave with others. Is there anything else that plays into this relationship building?*

MATT: How you communicate with the people you work with is important too. Some people might question whether admitting what you don't know will undermine your credibility, but I believe if it's done in the right way, then it does the opposite.

So I remember Bradley Wiggins once saying that one of the things he liked about working with me was that if I didn't know something, I would be honest about that, but then say, 'But I'll find out'. By being honest, I built a level of trust with him that he didn't have with everyone. My credibility in that relationship came from me saying, 'I don't know, but if it's important to you then it's important to me, and that's enough for me to be curious and try to find an answer'. If there wasn't an answer, the conversation turned to how we could make the next best decision with a lack of evidence, and go on that journey together.

A growth mindset and integrity are important, but so is how you communicate that to others in a way that builds trust and that they see value in. It's about how you walk side-by-side with people, particularly on these journeys when we know there's a lot we don't know. We're going after things that haven't been done before and we know it's going to be an emotional journey, so I have to think about what it will take for someone to want to walk with me on that journey and how I can be a great companion to them along the way.

MARC: *That leads us nicely into goal setting really. How do you make sure there's accountability behind those big goals?*

MATT: People use different terminologies, but it's important to differentiate between the dream and the objective. So, an athlete's dream will be to win Gold at the Paralympic Games, and we're all bought into that. But if I didn't do anything more with that, people would still be on the emotional journey, but in the absence of anything else, they'd end up pursuing their own agendas and motivations at their own pace. People would interpret that dream in a different way.

That's why it's important to then look at the objectives. You have to ask 'What are the objectives? What's that going to take?' And the answers will be different depending on where the athlete is in their career, their sport and their life. I also need to know what that dream means to them.

Really, you need to take that dream and identify the three or four things that are needed to achieve that—those are your objectives and they need to be tangible, accurate and aspirational. Getting the aspirational piece right is crucial. If you set it too high, it's demotivating, but if you set it too low, people don't push themselves in the same way and the progress you see will be slow.

In the context of high-performing teams, getting that right is hugely important for setting the tone for the team. If you can connect high-quality, very intelligent, motivated people to the right objective, it drives the team. As a leader, that enables you to shape, challenge and support the team without feeling as though you're out in front trying to bring everyone with you.

MARC: *I feel as though this brings us to the One Team Ethos, where everyone involved is supporting one another.*

MATT: Yes, you need that One Team Ethos and everyone needs to understand the objective; otherwise, they're just going to do their individual job. You need everyone to align their efforts to the objective.

An example where I have experienced this is the men's track cycling pursuit team at Beijing. At the time, we were struggling to break four minutes, and the Australians held the world record at 3:56.6. Eighteen months out from that Olympic Games, David Brailsford decided to change the coaching because we weren't creating a lot of change. So, we set a target for Beijing which was to achieve a particular time—3:53.3—over three seconds under the world record at the time. But we rode that in the Olympic final, which was an improvement of nine seconds in just 18 months.

I always maintain that it was the objective we set at the start of that process, and how we set it, that got us there. I still remember the meeting where we shared that objective with the athletes. We had to get the emotion right before we could land the logic, because the logic was a long way from where we were. So we brought the emotion and aspiration, but we'd also done enough work to be able to say, 'We don't have all the answers, but we believe we can get there'. This was where the philosophy around marginal gains really came to the fore. As an example, we really focused on training for the start—that first kilometre. At the time that meant a big change to how we were training, but everyone really bought into it and on the day it meant we'd almost won the race after the first four laps.

MARC: *Is there anything else that contributes to developing a high-performing team and ensuring everyone approaches these aspirational goals in the right way?*

MATT: I think you need clarity of purpose and the mindset that even the small things are really important, which is what underpins the marginal gains philosophy. It's also important to have a restless mentality around doing the difficult things now, if that's possible, because there's an advantage to not waiting, but you have to do that in a sustainable way. You don't want to set up an environment that's so restless and supercharged that you can't enjoy the journey and sustain the effort.

You've got to build resilience into your teams and your people. It should feel positive and motivating, as well as challenging and stretchy. You should feel like you're in a good, but not a comfortable, place. Everyone should look forward to being there, and that's what you'll see with the appropriate level of challenge.

That's where you can build excitement for the small things—the marginal gains. Too often people get excited about the big gains, but everyone is looking for those in any competitive environment and they're few and far between. That doesn't mean you shouldn't do them, but there is so much to gain from doing the small things because their collective impact can be huge. You want everyone on your team to know that no matter how small their contribution, it can add up to a significant leap in performance. For me, it's the commitment to doing the difficult things daily that sets high-performing teams apart from the rest.

When you're in a high-performing team, you feel it—in the environment you're in, in the way people operate and in the way they respond in that context. That means people will often see the context in which you're working change, and instead of waiting to be told what to do, they take responsibility for making those changes. At the same time, you're also able to see how everyone's different qualities and personalities are working to deliver that collective effort that allows you to achieve more.

MARC: *You've talked a lot about clarity of communication, goal setting and a growth mindset, but I'm also interested in the environment in terms of inclusion and psychological safety, particularly within the field of innovation...*

MATT: Within an innovation environment, you want to create a place where you can genuinely cultivate the power that comes from diverse perspectives. I love it on the rare times when you think you've really nailed something, and you take it to someone you know and trust who looks at it and reinforces that you've done a good job.

But then the next step is to take that to a diverse team and hand it over to them. This can be a really challenging interaction, but what you get back is, almost without fail, significantly better, and often brilliant. Getting that diverse set of perspectives on your work is particularly important when what you're doing is human-centric.

In an innovation environment in particular, where you're often trying to do things that haven't been done before, it's important that the culture of your team is such that everyone involved feels as though their differences are understood and valued. Such teams also need a shared understanding of how to work with differences within appropriate guide rails to ensure that there's enough consistency and commonality that things don't break apart. Often we get our confidence from having conversations with people about how we're similar. While that's still true in an innovation culture, we also need to have conversations around what makes us different so we can all recognise, understand and value the strength difference brings to a team.

MARC: *In your experience, what has stopped that working?*

MATT: Process being too dominant. Process is important, but it's the people who are going to get you there, not the process. For leaders it's therefore really important to understand how you can flex your process to enable people in your teams to do what you need them to do. In an innovation culture, you have to keep that design mentality and prevent it becoming more about the process than the people.

You might have done things the same way for years, but as soon as you get the sense that it's no longer right for the context or the people within it, you have to change it. It's also incredibly liberating for people within teams when you understand that mistakes are part of the process. We all know they'll happen, and when you can lead from a place of acceptance that they will happen, then people become less afraid of making mistakes and feel more able to try new ways of doing things.

We don't plan to fail in terms of the outcome, but the journey to get there is full of mistakes. The key is to recognise that and be confident with it, although it will never be comfortable. Leading through those mistakes is one of the best qualities of an innovative team. A sign of a true innovation culture is when things are going badly wrong and you see your team approach it with a level of confidence—they accept that this happens and decide what they're going to do about it.

Whatever innovation culture you want to build, it's important to keep talking about the qualities you want to see in your context for it to be more successful, and you need to deliberately notice those qualities in individuals and collectively. When you deliberately recognise the qualities you want to see, it reinforces what it takes to be truly innovative and drive high performance.

The three qualities that really stand out for me in our team are that they know how to hold a vision—when things get messy or go off track, they can come back to why they're doing what they're doing—they have courage and they have resilience.

My conversation with Matt covered all the attributes we've explored throughout this book and is a brilliant demonstration of how they come together to deliver high performance. There were lots of gems in there, but here are my top three takeaways:

1. *Be curious and keep asking, 'What don't we know?' Often this will lead to new opportunities for improvement and growth.*

2. *Consistently doing the small things well, even when they're difficult, is what sets a truly high-performing team apart from the rest.*

3. *Embrace mistakes as part of your journey. They will always happen, so use them to drive even more innovation within your team.*

One of the other things that came across very clearly throughout my conversation with Matt is that this is an ongoing process. Your work as a leader, and the work of the individuals on your team, will never be 'done'. There will always be something you can improve, and that mentality of seeking out those improvements, no matter how marginal, and making them will create a positive loop of high performance.

As Matt also pointed out, situations and teams change, as does the context in which we operate. We therefore have to adapt, which requires our people to have resilience to ensure that they can roll with change rather than resisting it. What is clear through both this conversation and the many others I've shared with you in this book is that when you take empowered people, put them in a supportive culture and provide them with defined processes in which to work, you can achieve incredible things.

Final Thoughts

High-performing teams are challenging to create and even more difficult to sustain. You may feel as though your job is never complete and you are probably right. There will always be something which requires attention. This is why I created my Best Teams Model, to act as a compass for you and your team on this journey.

If you would like to determine the strengths and areas of growth for your team, please visit my website at www.marcwoods.com/teams

Thank you for giving me your time and welcome to the world of high-performing teams—enjoy unleashing your team's power.

Notes

Chapter 1

1. Sorenson, B.S. (2024) 'How employee engagement drives growth,' Gallup.com, 20 June 2013 https://news.gallup.com/businessjournal/163130/employee-engagement-drives-growth.aspx.

2. Cloud, H. (n.d.) *20 Employee engagement Statistics you need to know | HR Cloud.* https://www.hrcloud.com/blog/20-employee-engagement-statistics-you-need-to-know.

3. PMI, (2016) *The High Cost of Low Performance.* https://www.pmi.org/-/media/pmi/documents/public/pdf/learning/thought-leadership/pulse/pulse-of-the-profession-2016.pdf

Chapter 2

1. Johannsen, R. and Zak, P.J. (2020) 'Autonomy raises productivity: An experiment measuring Neurophysiology,' Frontiers in Psychology, 11. https://doi.org/10.3389/fpsyg.2020.00963.

2. Metin, B. (2022) HR analytics: autonomy and employee engagement. https://www.effectory.com/knowledge/hr-analytics-autonomy-and-employee-engagement/.

3. Reichheld, A. and Dunlop, A. (2023) *How to Build a High-Trust Workplace*. https://sloanreview.mit.edu/article/how-to-build-a-high-trust-workplace/.

4. Grammarly (2023) *The State of Business Communication: New Threats and Opportunities | Grammarly Business*. https://www.grammarly.com/business/learn/state-of-business-communications-2023/.

5. Van Buggenhout, N. (May 2024) PwC, *The big power of small goals*. https://www.pwc.com/gx/en/issues/workforce/big-power-small-goals.html.

6. *Diversity and Inclusion White Paper: Hacking Diversity with Inclusive Decision making from Cloverpop* (no date). https://www.cloverpop.com/hacking-diversity-with-inclusive-decision-making-white-paper.

Chapter 3

1. Dallas, S.G. (2024) 'Patrick Mahomes is already thinking about his next Super Bowl win,' *TIME*, 16 April https://time.com/6966732/patrick-mahomes-interview-time100-2024/.

2. Savage, M. (2024) 'Taylor Swift breaks Wembley record and sings So Long, London as UK tour ends.' *BBC News,* 21 August. https://www.bbc.co.uk/news/articles/cr5nr3n6epvo.

3. An independent report co-commissioned by UK Sport and Sport England to examine allegations of abuse in gymnastics. The report was published 16 June 2022.

Chapter 4

1. PwC (2024) *Global Workforce Hopes and Fears Survey 2024*. https://www.pwc.com/gx/en/issues/workforce/hopes-and-fears.html.

Chapter 6

1. Elkins, K. (2018) *Berkshire Hathaway star followed Warren Buffett's advice: Read 500 pages a day.* https://www.cnbc.com/2018/03/27/warren-buffetts-key-tip-for-success-read-500-pages-a-day.html.

2. Dweck, C.S. (2007) *Mindset: The New Psychology of Success.* Ballantine Books.

Chapter 7

1. 1950 September, *Fortune*, "Is Anybody Listening?" by William Hollingsworth Whyte, Start Page 77, Quote Page 174, Published by Time, Inc., New York.

2. Gallup (2023) *The benefits of employee engagement.* https://www.gallup.com/workplace/236927/employee-engagement-drives-growth.aspx.

3. psico-smart.com (August 2024) *Enhancing employee engagement through effective use of internal communication tools.* https://psico-smart.com/en/blogs/blog-enhancing-employee-engagement-through-effective-use-of-internal-communication-tools-168198.

4. Gallup (2023) *The benefits of employee engagement.*

5. Asplund, J. and Blacksmith, N. (2024) 'The secret of higher performance', Gallup.com, 16 October https://news.gallup.com/businessjournal/147383/secret-higher-performance.aspx.

6. French, J. (2014) 'Towers Watson research study on effective communication and ROI', *Bizcommunity*, 3 October https://www.bizcommunity.com/Article/196/500/110632.html.

7. Wilding, M. (2023) *Overcoming your fear of giving tough feedback.* https://hbr.org/2023/07/overcoming-your-fear-of-giving-tough-feedback.

8. Herron, A. (2025) *Surprising employee turnover and retention statistics - WebMD Health Services.* https://www.webmd healthservices.com/blog/surprising-statistics-about-employee-retention/?tinypulseredirect=1.

Chapter 9

1. Kotter, J.P. (2012) *Leading Change.* Harvard Business Press.

Chapter 11

1. *CNET* (2002) 'Changing the culture at IBM,' 21 December. https://www.cnet.com/tech/tech-industry/changing-the-culture-at-ibm/.

Chapter 12

1. Scott, K. (2017) *Radical Candor: How to Get What You Want by Saying What You Mean.* Macmillan.

Chapter 13

1. *The importance of inclusion in the workplace* (2023). https://accionempresas.cl/content/uploads/principal-diversidad-equidad-e-inclusion-en-el-trabajo.pdf.

Appendix Assessment

To help get a sense of how your team scores on the Best Team Model, consider the definition for each attribute and the statement, which best describes your team. Make note on the model next to each attribute either 1, 2, 3.

Empowered People

Work Ethic: *The level of commitment, diligence and effort team members put into their work.*

1	2	3
Team members lack motivation, frequently miss deadlines and produce subpar work with little concern for quality.	Team members complete their tasks but lack consistency in diligence and commitment to excellence.	Team members take pride in their work, consistently go the extra mile and hold themselves to high-quality standards.

Autonomy: *The degree to which team members are trusted to be able to make decisions, take initiative and manage their tasks or solve problems independently.*

1	2	3
Team members constantly wait for direction, avoid decision-making and struggle with self-management.	Team members work independently but often seek unnecessary approvals or struggle with prioritisation.	Team members proactively tackle challenges, make informed decisions and confidently manage their tasks.

Integrity: *The extent to which team members act honestly, transparently and in alignment with ethical principles, even during challenging times.*

1	2	3
Team members hide mistakes, act dishonestly or prioritise personal gain over team success.	Team members generally act with integrity but may avoid difficult truths or take the easier route when faced with tough choices.	Team members are transparent, uphold strong ethical values and courageously stand by what is right even when not popular with others.

Growth Mindset: *The degree to which team members embrace challenges, seek feedback and continuously learn and improve.*

1	2	3
Team members resist change, avoid feedback and show little interest in learning or improving.	Team members are open to growth but struggle with setbacks or fail to apply feedback effectively.	Team members actively look for learning opportunities, embrace challenges and use feedback to drive improvement.

Defined Processes

Communication: *The effectiveness and clarity in how team members share information, listen to one another and adapt their messaging to different audiences.*

1	2	3
Communication is unclear, inconsistent, or ineffective, leading to misunderstandings and frustration.	Communication is generally effective but lacks adaptability, clarity or consistency across different situations.	Communication is clear, tailored to the audience and ensures alignment and understanding across the team.

Accountability: *The clarity of roles, responsibilities, and expectations, and the extent to which team members take ownership of their actions and results.*

1	2	3
Responsibilities are unclear, and no one is held accountable for failures or poor performance.	Some accountability exists, but expectations are inconsistent, and follow-through is weak.	Team members take full ownership, expectations are clear and accountability is consistently reinforced.

Goal Setting: *The process of defining, aligning and pursuing objectives that guide the team's work and measure success in line with their overall vision and strategy.*

1	2	3
Goals are vague, unrealistic or misaligned with the team's objectives.	Goals exist but may lack clarity, ambition or realistic timelines.	Goals are well-defined, strategically aligned and drive meaningful progress.

Recognition: *The extent to which team members' contributions and achievements are acknowledged and valued.*

1	2	3
Recognition is rare, and accomplishments go unnoticed, leading to low morale.	Some recognition happens, but it is inconsistent or lacks genuine impact.	Achievements are regularly celebrated, and team members feel genuinely valued for their contributions.

Supportive Culture

Resilience: *The ability of team members to adapt to change, recover from setbacks and support each other during challenges.*

1	2	3
The team struggles with change, lacks adaptability and becomes demotivated by challenges.	Team members can recover from setbacks but struggle with consistency or proactive adaptation.	The team embraces change, supports one another and thrives in the face of adversity.

Psychological Safety: *The extent to which team members feel comfortable expressing ideas, voicing concerns, and taking risks without fear of negative consequences.*

1	2	3
Team members fear speaking up, avoid risks and withhold honest feedback.	Some team members feel comfortable sharing, but others hesitate due to fear of judgment.	Team members openly share ideas, challenge each other constructively and feel safe taking risks.

Inclusion: *The degree to which all team members feel valued, respected and empowered to contribute their best work.*

1	2	3
Some team members feel excluded, disrespected or unable to share their perspectives.	Inclusion is acknowledged, but certain voices are still underrepresented or overlooked.	The team actively fosters a culture of respect, mutual understanding, and full participation from each member.

One Team Ethos: *The sense of unity, collaboration and shared responsibility among team members toward collective success.*

1	2	3
The team operates in silos, with little collaboration or sense of unity.	The team works together but still has divisions, with knowledge-sharing being inconsistent.	The team operates with strong cohesion, openly shares insights and collectively drives success.

About the Author

After 17 years as an international competitive swimmer, winning 12 Paralympic medals from five Paralympic Games, Marc turned his attention to high performance outside the world of professional sports. He has been advising the teams of global organisations for more than 20 years, working with senior executives to fulfil their own potential and help them realise the potential of the people they lead.

In an ever-disruptive world, Marc is typically called upon at times of transformation. This may come in the form of a new role and responsibilities for an individual, the formation of a new leadership group which needs to come together and define its purpose or a team which needs to shift gear to move to the next level.

As part of his work with executive teams, Marc creates and hosts senior executive events, building trust, gaining clarity on business objectives and developing collaborative team dynamics.

Intuitive and direct in style, Marc offers a sounding board to check and challenge thinking and behaviours. The ultimate aim is to gain clarity and build confidence in the decisions and actions being taken in order to enable performance at the highest level.

In addition to his coaching work, Marc is a motivational speaker and has written four other books in addition to *Best Teams*.

Personal Best, a combination of his inspirational life story and personal development advice.

Beyond the Call which, supported by research from New York University, looks at how to create conditions within an organisation that make employees more likely to go the extra mile.

Inclusion Unlocked, the definitive guide for business leaders to enable inclusion to flourish in their organisations.

Where Do All the Paperclips Go? A humorous look at the greatest business mysteries.

You can learn more about Marc Woods and his work at www.marcwoods.com.

Index